Eva's Story

Eva's Story

A Life Well Lived

Sylvia Heinze

XULON PRESS

Xulon Press
555 Winderley Pl, Suite 225
Maitland, FL 32751
407.339.4217
www.xulonpress.com

xulon PRESS

© 2024 by Sylvia Heinze

All rights reserved solely by the author. The author guarantees all contents are original and do not infringe upon the legal rights of any other person or work. No part of this book may be reproduced in any form without the permission of the author.

Due to the changing nature of the Internet, if there are any web addresses, links, or URLs included in this manuscript, these may have been altered and may no longer be accessible. The views and opinions shared in this book belong solely to the author and do not necessarily reflect those of the publisher. The publisher therefore disclaims responsibility for the views or opinions expressed within the work.

Unless otherwise indicated, Scripture quotations taken from the King James Version (KJV)–*public domain*.

Paperback ISBN-13: 979-8-86850-079-4
Ebook ISBN-13: 979-8-86850-080-0

Table of Contents

Dedication..vii

Introduction 1

Chapter 1   Childhood (1911-1923).................................9

Chapter 2   Youth (1923-1933) 39

Chapter 3   Early Marriage (1933-1943) 47

Chapter 4   Move to Detroit Lakes (1943-1952) 57

Chapter 5   Launching of the Older Offspring (1952-1962)..........65

Chapter 6   Just Three at Home (1963-1970).....................75

Chapter 7   Cast of Characters 89

Chapter 8   The Empty Nest and Beyond (1970-1979).............109

Chapter 9   Life After Vance (1979-1993) 131

Chapter 10 The Legacy of a Woman of Faith....................151

Bibliography...171

Acknowledgments...173

Dedication

To God be the glory that He provided life and strength for me to tell the tale of a spiritual woman. I pray that this story might encourage and enlighten those who read it. The ingredients in the recipe for a sacred life illustrated in my mother's story might be applied by the reader to better love and serve God in their journey.

This effort is dedicated to my family including my sister Shirley, who is my only remaining sibling who was able to be a part of the process of creating this volume. My husband, my main cheerleader, and our children and grandchildren were instrumental as well. My cousins, nieces, nephews, and other shirttail relatives (a term my mom was fond of using) have shared their love and appreciation of my Mom that shaped her story. The newest member of the clan, my great-great-niece, Lyra Gwendolyn Ruby Metcalfe, born October 24th 2024 1:07 PM 8 lbs. 1 oz, particularly inspired me with thoughts of my mother's wonderful legacy.

Lyra with her Great-auntie Jana

Carnegie Public Library, Detroit Lakes, Minnesota

Introduction

My mother, Eva Beatrice Larsen Sanford Schimming, was truly an amazing woman and an ardent bibliophile. Throughout her life, she was one of the regulars at the Detroit Lakes Public Library, a Carnegie Library that was completed in the year of her birth and is still open today. She devoured all the Zane Grey books she could find there or at the Salvation Army thrift store or rummage sales. She believed and espoused to everyone that she met that every day could be improved by reading. Finding a book on a knotty problem was generally the first step in finding a solution. All of her four children were steeped in the dogma of the magic of books and reading.

I had made some brief forays into publishing through professional scholarly publications and at some point, the seed of an idea to write a book to tell my mom's story was birthed in my psyche. Whenever the idea surfaced, I responded with "That will be my retirement project".

On the 8th day of my retirement, July 8th 2020, I began to review my mom's diaries as the basis for her story. I replied "I'm going to transcribe my mother's diaries" during my virtual retirement party when responding to the question "What do you have planned for your retirement?" Now, my statement hung heavy and seemed like a life sentence with no chance for parole. "Why was I so foolish as to say this, in front of witnesses no less?" I berated myself, but my conscience was pricked. Also, the fact that I had awakened at 2:30 a.m. and finally gotten up at 4 a.m., unable to go back to sleep, left me plenty of time at 5 a.m. with my prayer time and scripture reading behind me. Had God awakened me for this purpose, or was it the jambalaya? Suddenly, attempting to review my mom's diaries seemed daunting as I stared at the seven small volumes, spanning over two decades. Also, likely, I had not found all of them when I cleaned out my mom's house during the frequent Minnesota trips from 1986 -1988 to assist her husband Elmer after her stroke. There were, after all, still under bed chests that I had moved at least ten times in the almost three decades since her death. There could be more undiscovered diaries. "I should wait till I have them all before I start" my typical procrastinator voice declared. The sane part of me spoke up, "Stop it! You know that you likely have all or most of them so just get started!" After researching how to finish a dissertation in 15 minutes a day, I purchased a book in 2012 when I decided to get serious and finish my PhD before my 60th birthday. The book was purchased when I was surfing the web when I should have been editing, but that is beside the point! It was decided, I was going to start and work for 15 minutes daily.

My son, Adam had given me a tip to use the talk-to-text feature in my email to create a document that I could transfer to Word rather than investing $200 in software at this point.

The first diary volume, chronologically, was 1964. The 4¼"x 5½" cover of the less than one-inch-thick volume was a red leatherette. FIVE-YEAR DIARY was boldly impressed into the cover in Algerian font in all caps and highlighted in gold. The book that so intimidated me to open was held together with five strips of soiled, worn, white adhesive tape that had yellowed with age. I began reading the familiar, but at times, illegible characters penned by my mother in the five lines allotted for each day beginning with New Year's Day 1964. The words you see transcribed below are what my mother recorded in her diary:

Wednesday, January 1st

Watched Rose parade in forenoon. Went to Regiers. Watch night service with communion. Hackett's came in. Received picture of Winnie's family

INTRODUCTION

Thursday, January 2nd

Went to Sheridan's for dinner and Collins for early supper. Letter from Shirley and Howard.

Friday, January 3rd

Sylvia and I had haircuts at Beck's and went uptown blowing weather shampooed and set my hair (such a relief).

Saturday, January 4th

Vance and I went out to Ed's S. Bought groceries. Had chicken supper. Cleaned house while V went after wood with Reverend H. Watched daddy long legs

Sunday, January 5th

All of us went to S.S.& church. Darlene and Wally's for coffee. I went to YP & church. Mayme called Mama. Gave Robert Bowman the Bible

Monday, January 6th

Visited York's in the forenoon. Cashed mama's check. Went shopping at Penney's with rent money.

Tuesday, January 7th

Visited with Weston's with gift for Ronald Wayne and went back to mail scissors check & went to diamonds to shop furnace gassed. Bought Deanna's shoes

Five of my fifteen minutes was up. I looked at the barely intelligible information to start to edit. My original thought was to transcribe each word and using a respected qualitative research method, code and sort for themes. In my five minutes of trying to read my mother's illegible handwriting, I had already learned that this was a bad idea.

I decided to look more at the big picture. The inside front cover of the diary had the following words centered about halfway down the page

THIS IS MY PERSONAL
Diary
Mrs. V.C. Sanford

Her name was written in her characteristic handwriting. All this was covered up with a 2 ½ x 4-inch 1964 calendar ripped from a Stanley hostess party get acquainted spiral notepad with the ragged edge at the top. The calendar was held tenuously in place with two pieces of yellowed "scotch" cellophane tape, one at the top and one at the bottom. The almost sixty years since the tape was applied had taken its toll. The facing page was the 1965 calendar from the same type of notebook but they had either abandoned the spiral binding at this point or it had been neatly trimmed away. The same taping scheme was used but the placement was made carefully to allow the viewing of the saying just above the calendar "Memory is Elusive–Capture It". My manipulation of the long undisturbed page led to the calendar coming loose to reveal a box with the words "THE MIND Is a wonderful machine; it needs but be just refreshed and incidents can again be revived in their former clarity. A LINE each day, whether it be of the weather or of more important substances, will in time to come bring back those vague memories, worth remembering, to almost actual reality".

As I attempted to turn this page the aged tape reinforcement that had been added to the following page, between January 2nd and 3rd, gave way and the book lay splayed with the spine exposed. "Now you've done it! You should have never started this! You've ruined your mother's diary!" Sane Sylvia got a grip within a few minutes. Realizing that I was not dealing with archeological treasures but a source of information I forged ahead to view what was on the introduction "Five years of your life is in written form, will be your reward for keeping this

Introduction

book faithfully and accurately. You will record your daily habits, your thoughts, and events of importance. As you round up this chronicle of your doings, you will be able to check back a year from the time you are writing, and see at a glance your activities of a year ago. As you go along, you will be able to turn aside the veil of forgetfulness, and see the events of two, three and even four years ago. You will find amusing recollections that will bring chuckles – possibly business affairs whose record will provide valuable, and certainly little precious memories that you will want to keep in the permanent form which this book provides". I congratulated myself because even with time subtracted for my melt down, I was well over the 15 minutes that I had contracted with myself to spend.

Well, so much for the big picture. January 1st, 2022, I woke up and realized that I had written not one word in nearly a year and a half. By my calculation that would have been approximately 545 "I'll do it tomorrow" promises or maybe it was 75 "I'll start that next week" pledges. This startling revelation led me to sign up for a writing course that was free through our public library which began January 13th. "This is just what I need" I told myself in my new confident voice.

Lesson four in the course covered fears faced by writers. Fears identified by Ralph Keyes described what I have been concerned about in beginning the project of writing my mother's story. Keyes referred to E. B. White as a "gifted procrastinator". My gift is also procrastination. I intended to get a copy of Keyes book from the library before I began this assignment. Unfortunately, the day the assignment was due, was the first day I seemed to get around to it. There is no copy of the book in any of the branches of the county library. The book was available outside of our network. The book request process required 30 minutes. No one was sure when it would arrive. Since it was now the 11th hour and not even Amazon could get the book to me with their magic, utilizing the look-inside feature on Amazon was the only option. All of this is because I procrastinated! I am not as anxiety-ridden or fearful as Elwyn Brooks (E.B.) White seemed to be and he has had a very successful career in writing fueled by his fears. That was encouraging! One of the chapter sub-headings from the first chapter (not included in the seven-page sample) caught my eye, courage vs. fearlessness. Sadly, I did not have access to the book to explore more. Even more sad is that although I completed the course, I had not written another word in more than nine weeks. On May 28, 2022, I made a pact with a friend to be my conscience and meet with me weekly. The goal will be to finish the book by year's end.

About the first of October after three trips that had been rescheduled due to the pandemic and occurred in rapid succession and a personal bout with Covid for the second time, despite being fully vaccinated and boosted, I began to realize that the end of the year was not a realistic goal. My friend, editor, and saner person than I consoled me with the fact that she would send a copy of what I had completed to my children if I were to meet my demise before finishing the book. That seemed like cold comfort and I told her so! She laughed and remarked, "Whether you finish or not think of all the fulfillment you have received from the process". I had to admit it had been fun talking to folks who knew my mom and spending time writing and reflecting on her life. My mother's life spanned most of the 20th century with her birth just a year into the 2nd decade of the century and came to an end in 1993 with only 7 years remaining. The changes she was witness to in that time were incredible. The 20th century began without planes, televisions, and of course, computers. These inventions radically transformed the lives of people around the globe, with many of those changes originating in the United States. The century witnessed two world wars, the Great Depression of the 1930s, the Holocaust in Europe, the Cold War, revolutionary equality movements, and the exploration of space. Thinking about the opportunity to tell my mom's story with history, and a Minnesota flair gave me new courage.

The idea of a deadline is a necessary evil for a gifted procrastinator such as myself. New goal for completion: July 28th, 2023, on what would have been my mother's 112th birthday. The thought that with my August birthday, I had met my biblical expiration date, three scores and ten, startled me a bit. The thought which closely followed was that my mother had been gone for almost half of my life. Another tidbit that floated by, as things seemed to do randomly more often than I would like, was my memory wasn't getting any better.

As the first two months of 2023 unfolded, the chapter order and approach shifted but the project was moving along and the July 28th deadline seemed reasonable. Unfortunately, at the end of February, a close friend had a stroke. Fortunately, this friend had built a house on one level several years before, which greatly facilitated his recovery. This event prompted my hubby to insist that we consider other housing options. About March when we had exhausted the existing home inventory, we realized the only option was to build a home. The July birthday deadline for completion was set aside and we worked along thinking the end of the year seemed doable. Early August my editor friend was not feeling well and the malady resulted in the need for life-saving surgery at the end of August. We moved into our new home on September 5th. I was forced to face the reality that the end-of-the-year deadline wasn't possible. My resolve to work on the project grew stronger. My mother's story deserves to be told and I am enjoying the process, hence new dedication to finish despite the delay.

Sisters Evelyn and Eva circa early 1916

Chapter 1
Childhood (1911-1923)

The words of the 19th-century English nursery rhyme claimed to predict a child's personality based on the day of the week they were born. According to the poem's prediction, my mother would be loving and giving as she was born on Friday, July 28, 1911, and she was! The US Savings Bond was initiated in 1911 and I wondered if my grandparents received a savings bond as a gift to commemorate the birth of their first child.

This chapter, dealing with my mother's childhood, was daunting for me to begin. There are of course no survivors from that generation and her personal history is largely undocumented. Other than knowing that my mom was born at home, as everyone was, I don't even know where that birth was and who was present. She had no birth certificate which created problems throughout her life.

This led me to the idea of using sources from that period to extrapolate. For instance, hospitals were rare and not considered for use in birthing. This launched me on a research trajectory to fiction and non-fiction resources set in Minnesota or other rural areas at the time of my mother's childhood. While using these resources, my memory was triggered by events my mother had recounted. This combined research and recollection helped me to draw some conclusions about situations that I might include as part of my mom's story without being too far afield. Then I found myself getting mired in my research and I became a researcher rather than an author.

This quote from *Ready, Set Memoir!* by Lindsey Grant released in 2021 helped me "get over" myself and plunge in. "As much as you research and reflect on the past and produce realistic answers to bridge the gaps in the story, you won't have a solution to or reason for everything. Neither will your reader expect you to. In fact, proclaiming too much certainty can backfire and come off as inauthentic. Some ambiguity and lingering questions are important to memoir for they also represent the truth of memory, which is, in its essence, episodic, incomplete and impressionistic. With that in mind… you can leave well enough alone."

So here my dear reader I gave up my life as a researcher and became a writer. I humbly present my mother's story of a life well lived.

The second decade of the 20th century was described as a decade of industrialization and prosperity in agriculture in the Minnesota Historic Farm Study. In the year of my mother's birth, 1911, the most exciting event happened on December 14, 1911, when Norwegian, Roald Amundsen's expedition was the first to reach the South Pole. The world did not know about this important discovery until sometime in March 1912. I remember my grandfather, a proud Danish man, or Dane, saying that the famed explorer wasn't Norwegian but truly was of Danish heritage as the spelling of his name was Amundsen rather than Amundson, which was the common spelling for the Norwegian version of this surname.

Before my mother's first birthday, other news reports included many indications of battles that eventually added up to WWI. Further foreboding signs that major world changes were afoot were that Sun Yet-Sen, the father of Modern China, formed the Republic of China and within a month the last Qing Emperor abdicated at the age of six. The Titanic, the unsinkable ship, sank on its first and last voyage in April 1912. The thing that my grandfather most celebrated, besides my mother's 1st birthday, was that a Democrat, Woodrow Wilson, was elected president of the United States of America.

During 1913 there was good news and bad news for the people of rural Minnesota. Three events that were good news addressed the

Childhood (1911-1923)

transportation needs of the nation and the citizens of Minnesota benefited from these happenings. The first coast-to-coast paved highway, the Lincoln Highway, opened to traffic. The road ran just south of the Minnesota border. The first ship sailed through the Panama Canal, and railroads laid more lines. Improvements to the US Postal Service included the beginning of Rural Free Delivery which provided for mail delivery and packages to homes in outlying areas in the countryside. The bad news was the 16th amendment to the constitution provided a basis for graduated income tax, a source of constant vexation for my grandfather. WWI officially began in 1914. As the years of my mother's childhood unfolded the farm began to supplement horsepower with gasoline engines and the steam-powered threshing machines that visited the local farms during harvest. Designs of farm layouts and buildings were based on science and resulted in improvements in field drainage, barns with haymows, and silos. My grandfather subscribed to farm journals and was interested in progress in agriculture. My mother shared recollections of seeing her father read by lamplight with his precious glasses. I still have the glasses alongside his corn cob pipe on a shelf with the Larsen family photo today. Grandpa was known to have invested his time and money in new agricultural improvements quicker than many others who stuck to the old ways. Grandpa's brother, Jim, farmed nearby with Belgian horses.

On Thursday, February 25, 1915, my mother's next younger sister, Evelyn, joined the family group. "Another girl!" my grandfather might have remarked. The traditional interpretation of the English verse indicated that Thursday children have a long, successful life without limitations. The "far to go" in life I had always interpreted as a long difficult journey but literary resources indicated the true meaning was the child had a lot of potential. Grandpa could not see her potential as the barrier of her gender made him blind to the positive prospects. Grandpa was a bit disappointed as he would not have the farm hand or the person to carry on the family name he desired. The war was overshadowing many things on the home front. In 1916, the war news included the first use of tanks and the legendary Red Baron made his debut over the skies of Germany. In 1917, the Russian rebellion began and exacerbated the chaos and suffering caused by WWI. One headline read, "A million casualties for 5 miles of mud". Mati Hari, a courtesan and accused spy for Germany, was executed.

In 1918 WWI ground to a weary halt. The Spanish flu epidemic took the lives of 21,000 in one week in New York City. The Russian czar was deposed and his family was executed.

On Monday, October 27, 1919, the final sibling in the Larsen family, Mayme joined the family and she was as the poem foreshadowed, "fair of face".

The 1920 census for my mother's household indicated that at that time the family lived on rented land in Lake View Township of Becker County Minnesota on Detroit-Erie Road. The household listed with Hans F. Larsen as the head of household included my 32-year-old grandfather, Grandma 31, and the three girls Eva 8, Evelyn 4, and Mayme listed at 0 under the column headed age, so an infant. Also included were the two younger brothers of each one of the couple, Floyd E. McCulley, 22, and thirty-year-old James P. Larsen. This stimulated my thinking on how this number of individuals sharing the same small space impacted all the everyday activities of the family. The questions that arose were: had Jim been married and living with them after his divorce? Was Floyd there because he was sick and needed care or to help Grandpa with the farm work? Was that what had made Grandma so cranky?

During the 1920 census my father, Vance Sanford, was 15, the oldest of 7 children. His family resided in Hagen Township in Clay County Minnesota on a farm east of Ulen, Minnesota. I had always thought my parents both grew up near Ulen.

Circa 1920 several instances were appearing in the news about mailing children which provided my mother's fertile mind with an idea. My grandfather's family, except his brother Jim, lived in Iowa and my mother had a great affection for her Uncle Jewel and Aunt Lois, my grandfather's brother and his wife, who lived on a homestead near Algona, Iowa. At the age of nine, my mother somehow got the 15 cents needed to mail herself to Algona. She had done her homework and knew she came in under the 50-pound limit. Although she never actually mailed herself, I think this idea prompted a family trip on the train and was fodder for family jokes through the years. My thought was what a brave and interesting child she must have been.

Women's suffrage, the 19th amendment, was passed by one vote: that of Harry T. Burn, the 22-year-old representative from Tennessee. It seems the honorable congressman received a very convincing letter from his mother asking for his support of the amendment. This was a historical event that was oft quoted in the Larsen family with the admonition to listen to your mama. The very next year the first woman leader of the House of Representatives was installed. Hurray for early women's progress!

Before my mother's twelfth birthday, there was an Anglo-Irish treaty that partitioned Northern Ireland and brought joy to the Irish heart of Grandma Larsen, whose maiden name was McCulley.

Since I have no exact timeline, I decided to do a topical approach of themes likely related to my mother's childhood. There are one or more topics for each letter of the alphabet about the possible features of her childhood. The children of the early 20th century were definitely to be seen and not heard. Here are the ABCs of my mother's childhood:

A
Average

To be average or just a cut above Average is a common Minnesota desire. To quote Garrison Keillor in closing his radio program monologue each week on *The Prairie Home Companion*: "That's the news from Lake Wobegon, where all the women are strong, all the men are good-looking, and all the children are above average."

My mother enjoyed the stories Garrison Keillor spun about the mythical town of Lake Wobegon because it was true to her native Minnesota culture. Part of the culture is not to stand out but to have the quiet unspoken confidence that you are solidly rooted in the middle, perhaps just a cut above average, definitely not outstanding or unique in any way. The women being strong and no mention of appearance is very

Minnesotan. Vanity is not a thing in Minnesota unless it could be pride in their humility and being unremarkable. The men are described as good looking but certainly anyone would be shocked at the term handsome– much too showy. The grocery store in Lake Wobegon is named Ralph's Pretty Good Grocery and the Lake Wobegonians would shun anything called a supermarket.

Chester G. Anderson edited a book entitled, *Growing Up in Minnesota Ten Writers Remember Their Childhoods*. The general conclusion of the book is that Minnesota is a good place to grow up. He recounts many aspects of this Minnesota fixation with being average and lack of pretension in his introduction. "Not quite sublime, the scenery of the state has its own middle-of-the-road beauty. Even the wildlife of the state fits the image of moderation…earlier generations of Minnesotans who found the middling nature of the state to their liking…busily added their own temperate cultures. And we who continue to shape the middle-of-the-road image of Minnesota also like it that way. More or less."

The childhoods of the authors chronicled in this volume varied from the female-dominated native woodland experience of Meridel Le Sueur to Keith Gunderson growing up in a tiny Minneapolis apartment. The fact is the Minnesota average philosophy had a great impact on their writing, whether it was to escape in their recorded words to fantasy and excess or to mold the characters in their stories. The villains in the stories they created were tricksters and Easterners. We generally find no real heroes unless they are fictitious such as Paul Bunyan, just solid citizens plodding along. F. Scott Fitzgerald, a native son of Minnesota, was quoted as saying "Show me a hero and I will write you a tragedy".

Another perhaps more famous author, not chronicled in this particular book is Sinclair Lewis. The middle fixation comes through loud and strongly in describing activities in Gopher Prairie, the fictitious setting of his book *Main Street*, in reality, his hometown of Sauk Centre. The main character, Carol Kennicott, is based on Lewis himself. Kennicott's snooty New York wife makes repeated criticism of the void-like aspects of Minnesota.

B
Bath time

Bath time was the subject of several conversations that I had with my mother. Saturday night was bath night. The Larsen family were not churchgoing folks. My grandfather, Hans Ferdinand Larsen, did not work on Sunday out of respect for his neighbors who mostly were religious churchgoers and might disparage him if they observed him working on the Sabbath. "My beloved horses do need a rest" he justified to himself. In the typical Minnesota way, he needed to be average and fit in. Being average also required that he disavow the use of his rather pretentious name and was simply known as Fred.

On Saturday after dinner, the tub was set up in the kitchen and filled with enough water to get relatively clean. The water that had been laboriously hand-pumped from the cistern was heated on the stove. Dinner might have been an oven meal, not Grandpa's favorite, instead of the usual fried fare to have room on the stove for pots to heat the water.

The cleanest person, per my mother's recollections, or a special guest, would go first and all would use the same water. Usually, it was the children and women who went first. By the time my grandfather got in, the water was likely cold and not as clean. Grandma, not a kind woman but a rather sharp-tongued, spirited Irish woman might be persuaded to add some hot water to warm the bath. If she were having a cranky day, not likely. Bathtime was not the relaxing playtime that we think of today for children. Once or twice, I had the misfortune of being at their home on a Saturday night and my mother verified that my experience paralleled her own. Grandma Larsen would use her standard line "It hurts to be beautiful!" when she was scrubbing me with a brush and a bar of Lifebuoy soap. Grandma likely bought the Lifebuoy from a door-to-door salesman who handled it as one of his products when Lifebuoy was introduced in 1911 for home use. There was a big push for the use of soap to avoid infant mortality due to its germ-killing power.

Since the birth of my mother, her firstborn, my grandmother began using Lifebuoy and never stopped.

Once the hard freeze set in and the cistern went dry at the end of October or November until the thaw in March or April, the tub baths might be suspended due to difficulty dealing with the logistics of hauling and heating water. Other more demanding chores took precedence with the onset of the snow and cold. The fall/winter protocol was to put a small amount of heated water in a pan and wash "the stinky parts". The good thing was that this did not require a great deal of coordination and one could attend to their hygiene as needed. The summer, June through August, might have included "bathing" in a nearby lake. There were 412 lakes within 25 miles of Mom's home. She would just find a secluded lake and with her Ivory soap, which floated, bathed unsupervised without the benefit of the Lifebuoy germ killer and scrub brush, despite Grandma's reservations about this. The latitude being what it is, the bathing opportunity could go till 10 p.m. at the end of June. Mom mentioned that the mosquitos, leeches, eels, and other creatures would make the baths less pleasant. There was a component of fun in that there could be a great deal of water play and splashing. It was part of the rhythm of the ritual, and being good Minnesotans, they just dealt with it.

Grandma was the keeper of the bathing calendar, deciding when baths moved from a tub bath to partial personal bathing, or outside for the summer. She also acted as sentry, making certain that all bathers had the privacy they needed. Often families would bathe children together back then, regardless of gender (certainly, of the same gender) for efficiency, and perhaps allowed for some unsupervised playtime. But Grandma's sense of propriety caused her to make sure that all the girls had their bath time where she used her scrub brush and Lifebuoy liberally – definitely without splashing or any kind of fun. This was strictly about the business of getting clean.

Childhood (1911-1923)

C
Chores

My mother as the oldest girl would be responsible for her younger sisters. In community settings where neighbors worked together, oftentimes, for others' children. Sometimes there were chores to do that needed extra hands like making soap, butchering, picking berries, gathering eggs, feeding animals, making sausage, weeding, and many other tasks. Chores were assigned to the children based on age and ability to complete the work. Expectations were that the work to be done was done satisfactorily. If not, somebody was going to be in trouble.

D
Democrat

Politics in Minnesota is monolithic. You might not have a birth certificate but if there were one it would list Democrat next to sex. The Minnesota Democratic Farmer-Labor (DFL) Party was a force to be reckoned with. Later in her life, my mother's sister Evelyn was chairman of the League of Women Voters for the entire state of Minnesota. My grandfather repeatedly referred to this fact on every possible occasion whether it was appropriate or not.

E
Elephant

My mother recounted to me one of the great joys of her life was the elephants that came to town with the circus. The elephants were used to assemble the tents. As previously mentioned, the animals of Minnesota are mainly mundane. The big cats and fancy horses were thought of as frivolous but the elephants were admired by all. The versatility and usefulness of these immense creatures made them venerated by these hardworking common folk. Two groups of people did not attend the circus. The first and perhaps largest group had religious objections due to the scandalous, skimpy costumes of the performers and the general shadiness and lifestyle that seemed to be part of the circus. My mom and her family belonged to the second group that did not have the money to spend to attend the circus. My mother went early with her father to watch the elephants work in the early morning when the train unloaded.

F
Food

On one occasion when I might have been complaining about not having any more of my favorite cereal my mother tried to explain food in the context of her childhood to me–the central concern for all. Foodstuffs were raised through hard work in animal husbandry or grown in the soil of the fields or gardens. Chickens were primarily raised for eggs, and the tough flesh of the hens was only consumed slow-roasted to coax out all the tenderness possible after they aged and no longer laid eggs. One rooster was kept to fertilize a clutch of eggs for the hens a few times per year and to act as the daily morning wake-up alarm. Young roosters were most often the source of the fried chicken dinners. The chickens were free-range picking through the area for food and secured in the chicken coop only at night. One of Grandpa's major concerns was keeping the foxes or the raccoons out of the hen house. If he needed to get rid of the chicken predators, he did so carefully by setting traps on the perimeter or firing a well-placed shot to preserve the integrity of the pelt, which could be sold. There were cows and goats for their milk on most farms and again only butchered for their meat after their milk production had waned. The rich milk was the basis for delicious cheese and butter making. Fishing was also practiced but looked on with partial disdain as the results were unpredictable and had little to do with skill, but more to do with luck. Also, shiftless people would claim to be fishing but just taking a nap by the water. A few people hunted for pheasant, quail, rabbits, squirrel, deer, and other wild game to supplement their diets and protect their

Childhood (1911-1923)

valuable grain crops in the fields or storage. Folks living in the backwoods of Minnesota pretty much hunted what they wanted whenever they wanted as they were feeding their families. Although there have been game wardens since 1887 no one paid much attention to rules and regulations.

Although, Minnesotans are not known for their sense of humor there is a time-honored tradition of the Sven and Ole jokes. Sven and Ole are two fictional immigrants who live in Minnesota. They are characters used in jokes about any situation such as hunting.

Sven, a Swede, recently got promoted to Game Warden for his Minnesota district and was watching a beautiful flock of loons flying overhead. Suddenly, a shot rang out and one of the loons, the Minnesota state bird, fell to the ground.

Sven, cursing, rode his horse over to where it fell, only to see his lifelong friend, Ole, a Norwegian, picking it up. "Ole! Vat you doing??! You can't shoot da loon! De're endangered!! Dat's a federal offense! You'll be going to jail!!" Ole swore, "I taut it was a goose, I didn't know, oh, please tink of poor Lena! How will she get by if I'm in jail!? Please, Sven, I'm begging you!"

Sven agrees to let it go, but said, "Nobody can know about dis, Ole! Take it home and have Lena cook it up, eat it all and never tell nobody about it!" Ole agrees and leaves with the bird, wrapped up.

A week later, Sven runs into Ole and says, "Ole, you get rid of dat bird like I told you?" "Oh, ya, Sven! Lena cooked it up an ve ate da whole ting up. I put all the feathers and stuff in a bag, and burnt it." "Good," said Sven. "But I alvays vondered what da loon tastes like. How vas it, Ole?"

"Oh, ya, Sven, vas pretty good! Very tasty, kind of a cross between Vooping Crane and a Bald Eagle!"

F
Funeral

Since times were harsh, with illness and death frequent companions, Mom attended funerals with some frequency. Funerals were held in homes. There was no embalming and the timing of the burial changed with the seasons. In the hot months, the burial was expeditious. In the cold months with the frozen ground unyielding to the shovel, the bodies would be stored in the ice houses until the spring thaw allowed for burial. There is even a Sven and Ole joke about funerals. In this instance, Lars is an added character as he was sometimes. Lars is of Scandinavian descent as well so could have been Danish or Finnish as the name has ancient origins in Latin and is less characteristic of any specific nationality. The joke gets at the heart of the Minnesotan's feelings about death, similar to most of us, they would like to deny it.

Lars, Sven, and Ole were asked, "When you're in your casket, and friends and neighbors are mourning you, what would you like them to say?"

Lars said, "I vould like dem to say dat I vas a vonderful husband, a fine spirtual leader, and a goot family man."

Sven said, "I vould like dem to say I vas a vonderful teacher and servant of God who made a huge difference in da lives of people."

Ole said, "I vould like dem to say, 'Look! He's moving!'

G
Girl

My mother had two sisters. At the time she was born being a female exempted you from many chores on the farm. She never saw an animal being born although they had many animals that they raised. It was felt it was not good for girls to see "such things". The girls were not allowed to milk the cows. Probably many other homes that had boys and girls were doing a lot more work as the girls were likely allowed to go along with their brothers. When my mother was born it was important to have sons since many times they were used as farm hands. It was a disappointment to Grandpa that he only had girls. The girls were allowed to participate in learning to sew and other practical arts. My mother never did take to sewing and I'm sure that was distressing to her mother.

Games

In addition to inside or yard games such as checkers or horseshoes, there is a unique Minnesota game of snow tag called fox and goose. To play this wintry game, the oldest player, likely my mother, would tramp through the snow in the shape of a wagon wheel with spokes radiating from a stamped down four-foot circle like the hub in the center of the wagon wheel. This is home — a safe zone for the geese.

One child, likely an ornery boy that no one is fond of, is proclaimed to be "it" (*the fox*). The rest of the players are the geese. The fox chases the geese along the trails in the snow. All players must stay on the spoke trails at all times. Players cannot jump from one trail to a different one. Geese may run into home for a momentary rest where they will be safe. The fox cannot tag them if the geese are in the home circle. However, the geese cannot stay there very long. After a minute or two, they must leave the home circle.

The fox cannot enter the home circle and must go around the outside rim of the wagon wheel if one of the geese takes off on one of the spoke trails. The fox cannot tag any geese that are in the safe home circle. The fox must find a strategic location from which he can sprint to catch a goose. When the fox tags a goose, their roles are reversed. The goose now becomes the fox and the fox becomes a goose. The new fox begins chasing the geese trying to tag one of them. Play continues until a) everybody gets too tired b) everybody gets soggy, wet, and cold c) the fox gets frustrated because he can't tag anybody and he is "it" all of the time d) all of the above!

H
Health and Illness

My mother was a sickly child with crossed eyes. Illness was a major concern for everyone. If a health issue began it would often go from bad to worse and result in morbidity and mortality due to lack of medical care. Illness was a constant companion for most. Sometimes, a geographic treatment was the only option. My mother's Uncle Floyd (or Uncle Tubby, as everyone called him) moved to Colorado because he had asthma. He was a stout man with a garland of chins in the photos that I have seen. It was likely not the fat of a prosperous farmer that inspired envy in neighbors, but fluid retention related to heart failure exacerbated by his breathing issues. Home remedies that were used included ingredients like goose grease, turpentine, kerosene, onions, or other root vegetables. Alcohol was a common component in many concoctions. The remedies were versatile and could be applied as a poultice, inhaled, imbibed, or ingested. Sometimes the cure was worse than the disease and might have hastened the demise of many. Child safety was not a concern and there were many hazards for children with fire and primitive machinery with blades and gears as well as the Minnesota state bird, the mosquito, and many other biting and stinging insects.

When someone was ill relatives came to help when care was needed. My mother's grandmother, Granny, had an unnamed malady that rendered her speechless and invalid. My memories of her are being like a piece of furniture in the corner of my grandmother's or Aunt Jessie's living room. The menfolk would move her back and forth between the two households. She would be in the Twin Cities at my great aunt's home during the bitter winter months as they had reliable central heat, electricity, indoor plumbing, and running water.

Infection was a big risk. Sometimes people who had minor injuries on the farm would end up getting an infection and die from the infection because there was nothing that could be done.

Childhood (1911-1923)

Holidays

My mother loved holidays. Holidays were a big deal because families and entire communities would get together. Most of the everyday dinners were quick-fried meals, one-pot stews, or gruel that could cook all day on the wood stove, while the myriad of chores was performed. Only at the holidays was there time off from work and delicious food was created as part of the celebration. Some holiday traditions were dictated by country of origin. Mom's Danish family had rice with butter, currents, sugar, and cinnamon on Christmas Eve and New Year's Eve. There could be additional offerings of smoked fish if the budget allowed.

I
Imaginary Friend

My mother likely had a make-believe friend as described in Jesse Lee Brown Foveaux's story *Any Given Day.* Jessie Lee talked about blaming anything that went wrong on the make-believe friend. The imaginary friend could participate in games commonly played like fox and goose and could be projected to tag someone on your behalf when you were the fox and having difficulty tagging a goose through the usual means. An imaginary friend could also be the scapegoat for chores not completed, transgressions committed, or any situation where a child needed to explain away unacceptable behavior or improve their lot.

Ice Harvesting

Ice harvesting goes back to second-century China and has had many functions as providing for personal needs while keeping the waterways navigable in the cold winter months. The United States was the world leader in the commercial ice harvest industry. For many years ice was the second biggest US export with entrepreneurs who shipped ice to the southern United States and other countries around the world.

The ice harvesting industry began in Detroit Lakes in 1887, boomed through the 1930s, and started to taper off when electric refrigerators were introduced in the 1940s. It came to a close in 1970. Some communities, including Detroit Lakes, still do a historical ice harvest to get ice for building ice castles and sculptures for winter festivals. Some individuals who run resorts on secluded lakes in Northern Minnesota still do ice harvesting and keep an ice house to provide for their guests' comfort and food safety during power outages that are common during the summer storms. Most farmers worked the ice harvest to make extra money during the winter season at the commercial ice houses. Ice harvest was also like haying with their friends and neighbors to provide for their own needs for ice. The ice that was harvested was packed tightly into ice houses with sawdust or straw as insulation and would last a year until the next harvest if packed and insulated properly. Grandpa was an early adopter of all things technological so he was using an engine instead of horses long before other farmers in the area. They were getting ice for their own needs. Below is a quotation from the Becker County Historical Society about the large commercial ice operation where my grandfather worked to earn money:

"With temperatures hovering around 10 degrees below zero and a brisk wind coming off the frozen lake, nearly a hundred men work together, cutting fields, ribbons and cakes of ice weighing hundreds and hundreds of pounds to be loaded onto train cars and stacked in icehouses. It's cold outside, but they don't seem to notice as teams of horses plow snow off the ice, saw blades cut into the frozen lake and poles guide the ribbons of ice through a channel to the wooden tramway. As the strips hit the tramway, men with needle bars would break off the 22-by-32-inch ice cakes that were from 16 to 19 inches thick. The 400-pound ice cakes traveled along the tramway to the chutes, where they were loaded into the railroad cars. It took five men about 20 minutes to load a railcar. One man would guide the cakes off the tram and into the chute. Two swing men were at the railcar door to direct the cakes to the sides of the car where a packer would be waiting to guide the cake into place. Cakes that weren't loaded onto the railcars traveled along the tram to the ice-house, located where Holiday Inn is today, for storage. The ice along the channel gets slippery, with water splashing onto the edges as the ice floats through it. Some men have experienced the unfortunate feeling of slipping into the frigid open waters, only to be whisked off to a warming house to dry off and keep from catching pneumonia."

"It was something that kept you in groceries and whatnot. That was always good," Grandpa said. "Instead of having to sell some grain to pay for the groceries, I could work out on the ice. We had to eat". Grandpa spoke about his work at Addison-Miller Ice Company through the years. Ice harvesting was one of the largest industries in Becker County, with harvesting done mainly on Detroit Lake, though some surrounding lakes were also used for harvest.

J
Jokes

As previously discussed, in Minnesota the most common jokes were the Sven and Ole jokes. I heard this one from my mom, and likely she heard it somewhere during her childhood. Sven is Swedish and Ole is a Norwegian. Depending on what side of the nationality divide you hail from, Sven or Ole would be the hero or the dolt in many varied situations. Here is one of my favorites that leaves both lacking in the smarts department. It is not as much about the usual nationality bashing between the Swedes and Norwegians but has a jab at the city folks in Southern Minnesota using the usual characters.

Sven is vacationing at his cabin in northern Minnesota and happens to get in line at the creamery to get ice cream.

An Indian (Native American) man approaches him and makes a proposition.

Indian Man: Hey I have a deal for you. I will ask you a riddle. If you can answer it, I will buy you an ice cream, if you can't then you buy me one.

Sven: Sure, I like riddles.

Indian Man: They are my father's child but not my brother. They are my mother's child but not my sister. Who are they?

Sven: I have no idea. Who are dey?

Indian Man: Me! Good riddle huh?

Sven: Yes, a very good one.

So he buys the man an ice cream.

His vacation is over and he is back in southern Minnesota. He is in line to get ice cream at the local ice cream parlor.

He spots his friend Ole nearby and decides to try to get a free ice cream.

Sven: Hey Ole! I have a deal for you. I will ask you a riddle. If you can answer it, I will buy you an ice cream, if you can't den you buy me one.

Ole: Ok. I like riddles.

Sven: Ok den. Dey are my father's child but not my brother. Dey are my mother's child but not my sister. Who are dey?

Ole: I don't know. Who is it?

Sven: Some Indian guy up nort.

K
Kitchen

Minnesota people are believers that the best aromatherapy comes from the kitchen. Unfortunately, my grandmother was not a good cook. Gooseberries are one of the unique Minnesota florae. Gooseberries are an acquired taste. Grandma would create her signature dish, gooseberry pie, with a quart of gooseberries and a pound of sugar. No one likes gooseberry pie to be honest. Grandpa would suggest a stop at the creamery for ice cream on the way to the relatives to spare the relatives' taste buds and grandma's feelings.

Childhood (1911-1923)

L
Lakes

Lakes had a great influence on my mother's life as a child. The license plate of Minnesota has the slogan the land of 10,000 lakes. Once again, the Minnesota modesty kicks in as there are actually over 15,000 lakes over 10 acres in size. The mother of all lakes, Lake Superior, is splendid. In this case, the tribal name of Gitchee Gumee was trumped by the Anglo name Lake Superior. A number of the northern lakes are fifteen, twenty, and even thirty miles across. Most locations in Minnesota are no more than a few miles from a lake. Lake Itasca is the birthplace of the mighty Mississippi. There are so many lakes that unique names seemed to be a challenge for the average Minnesotan. Hence, 99 of the lakes are called Long Lake, 91 Mud Lake, 76 Rice Lake, 43 Bass Lake, and so on. Even within the largest city of Minneapolis, there are 20 lakes. There is disagreement about the exact meaning of the tribal word Minnesota which became the name of the state, but sky-blue waters seem the most believable. The interesting thing is that in most areas of the state, the lakes freeze solid and become roadways.

M
Music

To my knowledge, no one was musical or had any kind of music lessons during my mother's childhood. This was a bit of an anomaly in the still rather frontier-like area where music was a centerpiece of most celebrations.

N
North Dakota

North Dakota forms the north half of the western border of Minnesota. My mother told me that her father forbade her to play with a cousin visiting a neighbor because they were from North Dakota and "they are all Republicans", the Minnesota equivalent of an ax murderer.

O
Outhouses

My mother often remarked how much she loved our bathroom. When she was a child there was no indoor plumbing. Relieving oneself was performed in the outhouse which was a small shanty that was placed over a hole in the ground where the waste dropped into the pit. Some outhouses were nice and some were just a bench on the edge of the pit with no protection from the elements. One advantage of being in a family of girls was that the outhouse was nicer than most, although it was still scary to have to go to the outhouse at night. Sometimes the children were allowed to use pots in the house that were emptied during the daylight hours.

When the Sears catalog arrived, it was always a big event. They were precious and were hoarded by the adults. Everything, yes even houses for assembly and cars, could be ordered from the catalog. Once the catalog was outdated it would be used for toilet paper in the outhouse. Reading the catalog was a welcome distraction and exciting for the children to view as well as a comfy respite from the corn cobs and other vegetation that were normally used for wiping.

P
Play

On the farm where my mother grew up, there was a place where they put the old machinery so they could come and get parts if they needed it. In the spring or summer, my mother might sit on the seat of an old cultivator that was placed there under a tree. She also probably laid on her back looking at the clouds and imagining that she saw people, animals, castles, or other familiar or grand subjects portrayed in the cloud outlines. The girls also would likely find wildflowers and they would pick wild strawberries and blackberries in their seasons. In addition, Minnesota has various kinds of nuts that they might collect for play as well as a chore to bring to the family table.

The girls didn't have a formal playhouse but they would play under the trees or in the barn or various sheds on the property. They would likely bake mud pies and cakes in the sun and then set them on a makeshift table of a rock or hay bail. Weeds in old cans served as a centerpiece for their feasts. In the fall there would be jumping in the leaves. In the winter snow forts sprung up perfect for protection in a snowball fight. There were likely some heavenly snow angels as well.

Q
Quarantine

The practice of quarantine, as we know it, began during the 14th century to protect coastal cities from plague epidemics. Ships arriving in Venice from infected ports were required to sit at anchor for 40 days before landing. This practice, called quarantine, was derived from the Italian words quaranta giorni which means 40 days. State and local governments made sporadic attempts to impose quarantine requirements until in the late 19th century there became a federal law due to travel improvements. This Middle Ages approach was still the best option due to the limited knowledge and treatment alternatives available for infectious diseases. My Mom related some stories to me about long quarantines. Recent issues with COVID-19 have made me appreciate what a quarantine might have been like without Amazon. Truly frightening!

R
Religion

As a child, my mother's home was uncharacteristically devoid of religion and any religious practices. Religion was central in most homes and families, especially in the northern regions of Minnesota. Most services and community events centered on the churches.

S
School

Grandma always saw that her girls got to school and there would be a lunch packed in an old lard pail that they would likely share at school. If you were in trouble at school, you were also in trouble at home. Teachers and parents alike used switches and paddles generously to reinforce education. Sometimes there would be no school close enough so children would go and live with relatives that were near a school. Education was less valued than working the farm, and school was not mandatory, so many kids went without formal schooling, or had their educations cut short. The 1920 census form indicated that my grandfather had completed the 4th grade, spoke English, and could read and write.

Sisters

Being sisters was a problem sometimes because they would disagree and have different likes and dislikes. There was no allowance made for differences but all children were subject to the same expectations: to do what they were told and not question. My mother being the oldest suffered for any infractions of her younger sisters.

CHILDHOOD (1911-1923)

T
Trains

My mother did not travel often during her childhood but there were likely a few train trips. The mail, and everything else important, was associated with the train. They would go out and watch the train go by and sometimes the conductors would throw candy off the train.

She told me how fortunate I was to be able to travel when I was a child as she dreamed of going somewhere but the travel was very limited.

A special brand of trains was the orphan trains which began in 1854 and carried orphaned and destitute children and impoverished adults from the east coast into the west to find a new life. This resettlement system continued through the Civil War and World War I, finally ending in 1929. The Orphan Train Society of America began in 1987 and was instrumental in developing the National Orphan Train Complex located in Concordia, Kansas, 20 years later.

Minnesota became home to an estimated 6,000 orphans and impoverished adults as a result of the orphan train. One girl was born Edith Peterson six months after her father died in New York City in 1911. Edith arrived in Minnesota as a two-year-old girl in 1913. She was welcomed into a large family of seven brothers and four sisters. Edith Peterson Bieganek first learned of her personal history as an orphan train rider as a young teenager after her mother died. She had suspected based on schoolmates' comments but sensed that it was a forbidden topic. She learned her secret from a social worker who came to the family farm where her older brother and his wife moved in to care for the children still at home. "Two good things happened in 1929," she said. "The Orphan Train stopped and I went into the Convent." Sister Justine felt she had a good life but struggled with not knowing her heritage. "My parents wanted a blonde, blue-eyed, 2-year-old girl. It was like ordering from a catalog," she told a reporter from the St. Cloud Times. The 2010 paper highlighted the upcoming Orphan train reunion which Sister Justine was organizing at the age of 98. Sister Justine did find some peace in 1969 when she made a trip to New York and learned her birth name. At the age of 57, she began organizing reunions and searched for her one older brother.

Friends and relatives had suggested to my grandfather that he "order" a boy from the train to help on the farm after the birth of his third daughter but it was never pursued. Likely, Grandpa assumed that since they were not church people their application would not be reviewed favorably.

After the success of the Children's Aid Society's first orphan train, other organizations began sending their orphan trains west. Each organization had its way of doing things, but most orphan train trips followed a similar pattern. Before a company of children left New York, an agent visited the selected community two weeks before the placement. They arranged for newspaper advertisements, hotel accommodations, meeting locations, and a local committee. They would then return to New York to travel west with the company of children and at least one other agent. The agents of the Children's Aid Society and other organizations were individuals dedicated to the children in their care. They worked hard to find them good homes and to keep siblings in the same community if they couldn't place them in the same home. They checked on the children regularly and stayed in contact with them even after the children were of age. Being a placement agent was much more than a job to them.

The agencies knew they needed a system to check the backgrounds of potential foster parents. They utilized community members' knowledge of their neighbors to inform the agents about foster parent applicants. In the early years, the agent would select members of the local clergy to collect applications and advise them as to who would be good foster parents for the children. After some concerns that Catholic children were placed with Protestant families and vice versa, the agents moved from utilizing clergy to long-time citizens of that community, the town founders, influential members of the community such as bankers, merchants, doctors, lawyers, and elected officials often served as members of the selection committee.

These men (and some women) were responsible for distributing applications to interested parties, gathering the completed applications, advising the agent on which homes would be the best, and watching over the children after the agents went back to New York.

The placing-out meetings, where families could meet and select children to adopt, were held at churches, hotels, opera houses, meeting houses, schools, court houses, or anywhere to accommodate the large crowds that usually gathered for the event. The agent and company of children would typically arrive in the community on a Friday. Then they would take the children to a hotel to clean up and change clothes. The meeting would generally start mid-morning. At the meeting location, the children lined up on a vantage point. The agent in charge would speak about the mission of the organization, each child, and the expectations of the foster parents. Children were not "chore boys" or "kitchen drudges" they were to be sent to school, church, Sunday school, and taught to be useful citizens. Usually, there were far more applications submitted than there were children available. Those parties whose applications had been approved by the local committee could select a child to take home.

U
Uffda

Uffda or Uff da is a mild and polite word or phrase that is vocalized. Uffda is used instead of cursing when something is unpleasant, uncomfortable, hurtful, annoying, sad, or irritating. Uffda is the most common spelling when the phrase appears in print. The use in print is limited to dialogue with a Minnesota Scandinavian accent. There are a variety of spellings when it does appear in print including oof-*da*, *oofda*, *oofala*, *oof-dah*, *oofdah*, *huffda*, *uff-da*, *uffda*, *uff-dah*, *ufda*, *ufdah*, or *uf daa*. Uffda is a response when hearing something lamentable (but not too serious), and can be translated as "Oh, I'm sorry to hear that". The phrase is still used copiously in the Minnesota dialect and there is a whole industry around representations of the word in various spellings and forms on clothing, dishes, and wall art.

Ulen

Ulen was my father's hometown. Ulen has special significance to our family since we had relatives there and it was very near to where my dad grew up. During my childhood, we made frequent trips there to visit relatives.

The town is named after its founder Ole Ulen, who is buried in the old settlers' cemetery on the edge of town where my parents, brothers, and assorted other relatives are buried. These early pioneers were hardy, reliable people who were unafraid of the tasks that confronted them. Hardships were faced by one and all alike. Several times the grasshoppers devoured their hard-earned crops. Prairie fires were a menace. Sickness and death would strike and still, these undaunted pioneers stayed on. The population of Ulen has hovered around 500 for most of its life span. The types of businesses have changed but it remains an agriculturally based economy. Ulen is currently in a growth spurt as there is room to build new affordable homes with an easy commute to the Fargo-Moorhead area.

V
Vikings

Scandinavian roots run deep in Minnesota, and so does the belief among some that the first Vikings who inhabited the state were not of the National Football League variety. The theory that the ancient Norsemen explored Minnesota as much as 1,000 years ago blossomed after Swedish-American farmer Olof Ohman and his son discovered a 200-pound, rune-covered slab of stone in 1898 while clearing stumps near the rural town of Kensington. The inscription on the Kensington Runestone claimed that Vikings led by Paul Knutson had come to the prairies of western Minnesota in 1362 in search of the Vineland colony established by Leif Erickson, whom some Minnesotans believe also visited the state. Further corroboration occurred in 1911 when a farmer near Ulen while plowing, heard the sound of scraping metal. He discovered what appeared to be an iron bar. Upon closer inspection he noticed carvings and once thoroughly cleaned, he saw that it was a sword that is believed to have dated back to the expedition led by Paul Knutson in the 14th century.

W
Weather

My mom told me that people in Minnesota prepare for winter as if it were a war. A common joke in Minnesota is that there are only two seasons, winter and road construction. Winter does wreak havoc on the roads. Minnesota's climate has done much to shape the state's image and culture. Minnesotans boast of their "theater of seasons", with a late but intense spring, a summer of watersports, a fall of brilliantly colored leaves in the hardwood forests, and a long winter made bearable by outdoor sports and recreation.

Two of the three brief seasons besides winter have their brands of problematic weather. Spring has its flooding and summer its heat which breeds tornadoes and thunderstorms. The mellowness of autumn cannot truly be enjoyed as it is a race against the clock to be prepared for the ominous impending onset of winter. When autumn wanes too quickly, and winter comes too soon, the vulnerability that ensues can be deadly. Minnesota has extreme weather as evidenced by these records.

Highest Temperature 115 °F (46.1 °C) July 29, 1917, Beardsley
Lowest Temperature –60 °F (–51.1 °C) February 2, 2018, Tower
Largest single-day change 71 °F (39 °C) April 3, 1982, Lamberton

XYZ

My mother used a common Minnesota expression she learned during her childhood on me more times than I can count. "That is the XYZ". The term XYZ means the end and everything had been included. There will be no further discussion.

Sisters Evelyn and Eva circa 1926

Chapter 2
Youth (1923-1933)

The process of writing this book has led me to believe there is much more that I don't know about my mother's life as a youth than what I do know. Other than a few photos there is no link to that time in my mom's life. Reading about the history of Minnesota farming did provide some perspective. The farm in my memory, where my grandparents resided, was the farm where my mother lived with her parents during her youth. The subsistence farm of maybe 80 acres northeast of Detroit Lakes was rented and the purchase came about after the Depression, possibly as a part of a 1936 government land grant program. There are so few details that I can be sure of that I feel a need to apologize for my lack of knowledge and just be honest and identify most of the content of this period in my mom's life as pure unadulterated, speculation. I intend to share my mom's story not necessarily to provide an accurate historical record. Hence, I have ignored my scholarly urge to do extensive research. Such research might have answered my questions but would not add to the story and only delay the completion. Remember my gift is procrastination. Now, with this caveat, I will unapologetically reflect on the possible youthful period experiences of the person that many knew and loved.

From the time my mom was 12 the rural Minnesota culture would dictate that she would have been considered capable of most tasks the same as an adult woman. There was no such thing as teenagers or preteens in 1923. All womanly concerns such as menstruation and childbearing were cloaked in mystery until the need to know catapulted itself into your life. You worked and helped your family as best you could despite whatever responsibilities or inconveniences you might have. The old story about women giving birth in the fields and going right back to work would be the standard.

If you lived in a rural Minnesota area as a youth it was likely a life of isolation. There was a lot of work and no time for "foolishness".

In Minnesota's agricultural history, the roadways were pinpointed as one of the causes of isolation. The rural roads were built and maintained by townships which meant clearing trees by hand and then dragging one of the larger logs you had just cleared with a horse to smooth it. When the roads filled in with snow in the winter, they became paths for sleighs. In the spring when the ice pack from the sleigh traffic melted, it turned the road into a muddy morass. Although cars were becoming popular in other places the roads made them less prevalent in this area. Outings off the farm were limited to rare holiday excursions and necessary trips to pick up supplies or deliver products to market.

The radio was a revelation and came about in my mom's early youth. There was likely no electricity on the farm at that time. Linda A. Cameron, program manager for the MNopedia project at the Minnesota Historical Society, wrote an article in 2010 that illuminated some facts about rural electricity in Minnesota. As early as 1914 there were pockets of rural electricity but none in northern Minnesota. The 1930 census reported 185,255 farms in Minnesota with 895,349 people living on them. Of that number, 23,342 farm homes had gas or electric lighting. Most families used kerosene lanterns in their houses and outbuildings and lived without indoor plumbing. Even so, by 1934, 6.8 percent of Minnesota's farms had central station electrical service. As a result, less than 11 percent of American farms had electric service in 1935 compared with 90 percent of city residents. My mother's family would likely have enjoyed listening to the radio with relatives or friends who lived in town.

The years of my mother's youth, from age 12 to her marriage in 1933 had several significant or interesting events in history that impacted her personal life. The event in the news that spanned her youth was

King Tutankhamun's tomb. King Tutankhamun was commonly known as King Tut. The unfolding events likely fascinated my mother. After a year of finding and excavating the entrance to the tomb in 1923, the year my mother turned 12, the Burial Chamber was opened by life-long Egyptologist, Howard Carter. The excavation and cataloging of the tomb took about 10 years and was completed before the end of 1932.

In 1924 the first Macy's Thanksgiving Day parade was held and likely was listened to on the radio in the store that sold radios as a promotion, or, in someone's home. During the diary years (1964-1986) of my mother's life the tradition of watching the Macy's parade on television was made possible by a gentleman from Scotland, James Logie Baird. In 1925 Mr. Baird held the first public demonstration of the television set he had invented.

In 1926, F. Scott Fitzgerald, a Minnesota boy, who wrote about the flamboyance and excess of the prosperous 1920s, published *The Great Gatsby*.

Though the famous aviator Charles Lindbergh was not technically a Minnesota boy as he was born in Detroit, Michigan, he spent most of his childhood in Little Falls, Minnesota. He was even more beloved by my family due to his heritage. Lindberg's father was a Minnesota Democratic Farmer Labor party politician.

My parents' courtship began in 1928 while my mother was in high school. My father was working and owned a car. Dad brought his cousin, Roy Coalwell, or Stub as people called him because of his height, to pick Mother up for a date. This was a combination of Roy's last date and Mom and Dad's first date.

The stock market crash in 1929 ended the decade of progress and prosperity and plunged the country into economic depression. The stock market crash had financial repercussions for everyone. The depression was likely the reason my mother and father waited some years to get married as they needed to help their respective families.

My mother graduated from high school in the class of 1931 which made her 19 almost 20 by the time she graduated from high school. She was well beyond proper marriageable age but likely the economic situation delayed their nuptials. My mother went to teacher's training to be able to earn some money to help her family save up for their marriage. My efforts to find specific information on the length, content, and origin of her training were not successful. It was likely a 6-week course that was offered as an extension of Moorhead State Teachers' College. The four-year degree program on campus at Moorhead State was described as a program to prepare school administrators and seemed to have only males in the photos I found. There was recognition that the teachers who were recruited from the East Coast were generally not within the reach of rural one-room schools and the rigors of life in the north resulted in a succession of teachers in a brief period. One author, Laura Ingalls Wilder, described her experience as a teacher in a one-room school in her book *The Long Winter*. Two months before her 16th birthday, Ingalls accepted her first teaching position. She later admitted she did not particularly enjoy it, but felt a responsibility from a young age to help her family financially, and wage-earning opportunities for women were limited. As with my mother, her teaching career ended with her marriage. Unlike Wilder, my mother graduated from high school and had some formal training before beginning to teach. Many schools also served as the local chapel on Sundays, and evening/Saturday meeting places for local people and activities. Being mostly rural, many schools had no plumbing or sanitation. Teaching standards often varied from school to school as the teacher was compelled to coach children of all ages/grades within one room regardless of their area of main competence.

There were only a few places in the world where one-room schools existed. Norway and Sweden were countries where one-room schools were prevalent. The Scandinavian settlers brought thorough knowledge of how to build, plan, and support a school with them when they came to Minnesota. The quality of facilities at one-room schools varied with local economic conditions, but generally, the number of children at each grade level would vary with local populations. Most buildings were of simple frame construction, some with the school bell on a cupola. In some locations, the schoolhouse was painted red, but most seem to have been white. There is a photo of a white school with a cupola that I assume to be the school where my mother taught. My father was likely the photographer.

The teachers who taught in the one-room rural schools were very special people. During the winter months they would get to the school early to get a fire started in the potbelly stove, so the building would be warm for the students. On many occasions they would prepare a hot, noon meal on top of the stove, usually consisting of soup or stew of some kind. They took care of their students like a mother hen would care for her newly hatched chicks, always looking out for their health and welfare.

A typical school day was 9 a.m. to 4 p.m., with morning and afternoon recesses of 15 minutes each and an hour for lunch. The older students were given the responsibility of bringing in water and carrying in coal or wood for the stove. The younger students would be given responsibilities according to their size and gender such as cleaning the blackboard (chalkboard), taking the erasers outside for dusting plus other duties that they were capable of doing.

My future step-father, Elmer Schimming, was nine years younger than my mom. His family did not own any property and lived a hardscrabble life as farm laborers. Elmer was one of the older children and there was no emphasis on education in his family. My mom and Elmer were married for three years before I discovered he could neither read nor write. It seems that he only made it through the third grade, despite his desire to learn. Elmer was a large and sturdy boy and never went to school until after his morning chores were completed and there was nothing further, he could do that day to contribute to the family income. He likely did not have proper clothing or a lunch and was one of those who benefitted from the teacher's ministrations to his needs and those benefits may have accounted for his desire to go to school despite great barriers. The Schimming family had inadequate housing and moved to where the work was and no one took the trouble to enroll him in school if there was a move.

Most students walked often up to three miles to school. The school board or families might provide transportation for children who lived further away. Transportation was often in the form of a horse-drawn sulky, which could only travel a limited distance in a reasonable amount of time each morning and evening, or students might ride a horse, these being put out to pasture in an adjoining paddock during the day.

The schoolhouse was the center and focus for thousands of rural communities, hamlets, and small towns. Often, town meetings and picnics were also held there. My mother taught for about two years from 1931 till 1933–likely why their wedding was on May 28th, the end of the school year.

The kidnapping of Lindbergh's infant son in 1932 was a tragedy that was in the news from March through May. The boy's body, which showed evidence of murder months before, likely at the time of his kidnapping, was discovered near Lindbergh's New Jersey home in May. My parents, anticipating their marriage, would have been especially impacted by this sad news about their Minnesota hero. Perhaps the economic situation had improved enough but also it was possible that the urgency for marriage increased because of these sad events and there was a year to make plans.

Mom and company having fun while working in a shoe cleaning laundry extravaganza.

Eva and Vance Sanford, The Newlyweds, June 3rd, 1933.

Chapter 3
Early Marriage (1933-1943)

On Sunday, May 28th, 1933, my mother wearing a dark suit, without even a corsage, went to the parsonage of a nearby tiny independent church bright and early before church started with her intended groom. The minister, who was essentially a stranger, was likely the only one willing to perform a wedding ceremony without some denominational formalities. My parents, who espoused no particular faith, would have been married by the justice of the peace but Sunday was the only day my father was off from work. The simple brief ceremony occurred without any attendees besides the pastor's wife, who served as a witness. There was no photograph. There was a reception later at the homestead of the Sanford family as pictured above.

Several questions went through my mind about the nuptials. I wondered why we didn't discuss any of these things when I got married. Since the weddings of my mother's sisters were simple as well, I thought this was just how weddings were in the 1930s. When I did a little research, it seemed there were fancy weddings. Fashion was taking inspiration from the silver screen and wedding gowns were no different. Wedding gowns featured in the movies were designer-made and affordable only to the rich, but that didn't stop knock-offs from being offered to brides at a fraction of the price. White or light-colored party dresses were recreated as wedding gown patterns for brides-to-be, making the latest designs attainable for all budgets. My grandma Larsen had a wedding dress and a formal portrait when she got married on November 9, 1910. Not sure if the depression had hit so hard or if any lack of church affiliation, sewing ability, and time all added up to the minimalist merging. It was not uncommon for men and women alike to have only one good outfit and likely what my mother was married in was that outfit.

The couple made their first home in an apartment on the banks of the Red River of the North in Moorhead, Minnesota. The apartment would have been close to the trucking depot but far away from home for both of the newlyweds, who had lived with their parents up until this time. That summer a record-breaking drought caused the soil to be blown away by the wind creating the Midwest dustbowl.

My parents' first child, Barbara Jane, was born in the upstairs apartment of Mrs. Thompson, a neighbor and friend. Their darling daughter was born Monday, February 12th, 1934, and all agreed that she was fair of face. There are no vital statistics such as weight and length or time of day that I could find. Mrs. Thompson served as a midwife for many and one of the reasons was that she had a 2nd floor apartment that didn't need to be evacuated during a flood.

The flood didn't come till April that year. At the end of the chapter are photos of the neighborhood where they had their apartment after the floodwaters had receded. Imagine having a two-month-old child and needing to evacuate your home and then return to clean up the muddy mess. The Red River of the North forms the border between North Dakota and Minnesota. In northwestern Minnesota, water flows north by way of the Red River of the North and the Rainy Rivers into Canada's Lake Winnipeg and on to Hudson Bay. The watershed of the Red River of the North lies largely on flat prairie land. Riverbanks are low and currents are sluggish. Minnesota's north-flowing streams are particularly prone to spring flooding. Conditions that contribute to flooding are created when runoff from melting snows and warm rains in the southern part of the watershed reach northern areas still frozen over or clogged with ice flows. The choice to live on the banks of the flood-prone river was based on the fact that the rent cost would have been low. The drought of the summer before meant there wasn't as much vegetation to slow runoff and prevent flooding. This coupled with the melting snow and higher-than-normal rainfall caused the river to overflow its banks. The first year of my parents' marriage came to a close.

There was some good news for the grandparents besides the birth of their first grandchild in 1934. U.S. Senator Henrik Shipstead of Minnesota understood his rural neighbors' desire for affordable electric service. On a selfish note, he too wanted service for his cabin on Lake Irene in Douglas County and advocated in Washington for reasonable rates for rural customers in 1934. He gained the support of President Roosevelt, who created the Rural Electrification Administration. On May 11, 1935, President Franklin D. Roosevelt signed Executive Order 7037 to create the Rural Electrification Administration (REA), a New Deal public relief program. The program provided $1 million for federal loans to bring electric service to rural areas. It revolutionized life in rural Minnesota and across the country.

The lack of support from commercial power companies prompted groups of farmers to work together to organize electric cooperatives. Each co-op's board of directors drew up articles of incorporation and bylaws and registered with the State of Minnesota. My outspoken grandmother Larsen worked ceaselessly to promote the REA because they encouraged the inclusion of women directors. Rural electrification has had a huge impact on Minnesota's farm economy and the rural standard of living. Electricity found many uses on farms that helped to increase productivity, raise farm income, and boost the local economy. Farmers could use the money from REA loans to purchase milking machines, cream separators, bale lifters, and other electric equipment and tools. The loans also covered the installation of indoor plumbing and the purchase of such labor-saving household items as refrigerators, washing machines, and electric irons. An early Minnesota REA co-op, the Douglas County Cooperative Light and Power Association was incorporated in November 1935. On July 1, 1936, the co-op received a $50,000 REA loan at 2 percent interest to build fifty-six miles of power lines. Electricity reached the first forty-five farms – and you guessed it, Senator Shipstead's cottage – in September 1937.

Eva's Story

On Saturday, April 4, 1936, my aunt Evelyn married Palmer Onstad and moved close to my parents. My mother commented how happy she was to have her sister nearby.

Worldwide poverty encouraged the development of fascism and Nazism.

One ray of hope, the man who would become the outstanding athlete, Jesse Owen, delivered a blow to Nazism with his athletic prowess. Jesse set three world records and tied a fourth in track and field at a Big Ten Conference meet in 1935 when he was at Ohio State. This feat is still referred to as the greatest 45 minutes in the history of sports. Jesse was born the youngest of 10 children to a sharecropper in Alabama. His grandfather was a slave. He was just two years younger than my mother and he lived till 1980 so my mom followed his career and loved his story of his rise from poverty and obscurity despite his race to become recognized worldwide. His family moved to Ohio when Jesse was nine. They were part of the great exodus of blacks from the segregated South looking for opportunities that promised a better life in the industrialized North. While his father and older brothers worked in a factory, Jesse went to school and learned not only the standard subjects but also that he had a passion for running. His talent was recognized and encouraged by his family and further developed by his junior high school track coach. Jesse Owens won four gold medals at the Olympics held in Germany and thwarted the myth of Aryan superiority right in Hitler's backyard. Some advised that he should not go due to racial tension but in truth, he was treated better in Germany during the Olympics than after his return. Following the ticker tape parade in New York honoring the Olympic athletes Jessie and the other black Americans were required to use the rear entrance and freight elevator at the Waldorf Astoria Hotel where the reception was held. Jimmy Carter delivered a fitting tribute after his death "No athlete better symbolized the human struggle against tyranny, poverty, and racial bigotry."

My sister, Shirley Ann, was born at St. John's Hospital in Fargo, North Dakota, on Sunday, August 9th, 1936. The nursery rhyme of British origin has the most to say about the child born on Sunday: "And the child that is born on the Sabbath day is bonny and blithe, and good and gay."

In later years I learned that in the space between my oldest sister and her younger sibling was a miscarriage. Perhaps that is why the hospital was resorted to for Shirley's birth. The day Shirley was born was the very day that Jesse Owens won his 4th gold medal in the 4 X 100 relay. Interestingly, Jesse Owens and his college friend, Ralph Metcalfe, were last-minute substitutes for some Jewish American runners. It was thought a move to placate Hitler as both Owens and Metcalfe had already won medals and they did not want to add insult to injury with the issue of the Jewish runners likely receiving a gold medal. There was also speculation that there was an anti-Semitic individual who had the power to make this change and was secretly a Nazi sympathizer. Through the years the Olympic committee tried various ways to make amends to the individuals for this controversial decision that impacted their lives.

Hubert Vance was born only 11 months behind his sister born on Tuesday, July 13, 1937. As Tuesday's child, he was full of grace according to the poem. Hubert was also born at the hospital. Hubert was the first grandson on both sides of the family. It was a happy day to have a son for my father and despite his frugal nature he splurged and bought cigars to pass around to his trucking buddies.

Evelyn and Palmer had a son born on Friday, August 27, 1937. He and his cousin Hubert were very close in age and always had a special bond as they had many opportunities to be together in these early years.

Amelia Mary Earhart disappeared over the Pacific Ocean in 1937 during a circumnavigation flight attempt. The family's fixation with aviation and pride in the accomplishments of strong women received a saddening blow that day. My Mom used to optimistically say, "I hope Amelia is living somewhere happily on an island".

In 1938 Orson Welles' radio adaptation of *The War of the Worlds* is broadcast. Likely, many relatives would have come to my parents' home to enjoy the broadcast but I never heard any direct references to this event.

On Saturday, November 4th, 1939, mother's youngest sister married her soldier sweetheart Ray Anfinson, on Veteran's Day in Hawley, Minnesota. The young couple lived there with Ray's folks. Hawley was exactly halfway between Detroit Lakes where the three girls' parents lived and where Mayme's two older sisters lived so I am sure there was much visiting that went on. Mayme had worked as a cook for the Governor of North Dakota from sometime after her high school graduation. Her friend Amy was the governess and the girls had great fun traveling with the family. But Mayme missed her family and was glad to be able to be close by once again after her marriage.

When Germany attacked Poland in 1939 it served as the official kickoff for World War II. I remember Grandpa Larsen talking about a neighbor who was from Germany bragging that Germans would be in charge of the world soon. The people of this rural area watched as county after country was invaded and feared that their neighbor's prediction might come true.

Early in 1940, the Germans occupied Denmark after only a six-hour skirmish. The German government was not all that interested in Denmark but needed Denmark as a strategic location to launch an attack on Norway. It must have broken my grandfather's heart. There were still many of his family in the old country and he feared for their safety.

Despite concerns about the war Americans were gradually beginning to feel better as they were becoming more prosperous and leaving the deprivation of the depression behind. Farm owners could work a lifetime with little discretionary income and the saying "he bought the farm" meant that he died and the life insurance paid off the farm. Workers in the new factories springing up now earned up to the previously unprecedented $1,250 per year. This new environment fueled the making of the great movie "Gone with the Wind". Jazz sounds were the popular music of the day from the likes of Benny Goodman and Count Basie amongst others. The invention of nylon stockings the previous year was all the rage with women and people had time to turn their thoughts and money to things such as fashion.

Early Marriage (1933-1943)

Mayme and Ray had four sons in rapid succession. Raymond Sydney was born on February 2nd, 1941 and his brother, David "Andy" joined him just over a year later on February 27th, 1942. Burton Chester was born on January 9th, 1943, and his brother Michael Phillip joined the family on November 19th, 1943. Four boys three and under for a few months. Whew!

Palmer and Evelyn had their daughter, Joanne, on October 25th, 1942 sandwiched in between the Anfinson boys.

My parents may have experienced another miscarriage or two as I believe someone once said that my mother had a dozen miscarriages all totaled.

In 1941 outside of America things were not good as Germany invaded France which meant that between Germany and Italy, most of Western Europe was controlled by Nazi Germany or Fascist Italy except for England. FDR was elected for a third term and Americans were starting to believe they should help Britain in its fight for survival with Germany. The first peacetime draft occurred in September which had ominous overtones for the future. My Dad was deferred from the draft as his job in trucking was considered necessary. Britain was being bombed incessantly and many believed it may only be a matter of time before America would be involved. The United States maintained neutrality until December 7th, 1941, when the surprise attack on Pearl Harbor plunged the US into World War II.

The war in Europe continued to dominate world affairs. Many cousins and neighbors were drafted. The first peacetime draft began in 1940 and the draft age had been dropped from 21 to 18. Many young men went to war, even before the Japanese surprise attack on Pearl Harbor which killed 2400 Americans and caused the United States to abandon neutrality. The British Prime Minister Winston Churchill addressed the joint session of Congress asking for help in the form of arms but none were provided until after Pearl Harbor.

Otherwise, life continues as usual. The Vance Sanford family was left to try to assist the families left behind when the menfolk went off to serve their country. Their enlistments were specified only as "the duration of the war". Dad worked long hours at his full-time job which likely earned him a salary of around $145 per month. One of Daddy's side jobs was to deliver films to movie theaters and likely the Sanford children were able to enjoy "Dumbo" at that theater on complimentary tickets Daddy received. He also needed to help out on the Sanford family home farm and his in-laws' farm as there were no able-bodied men to hire. They had been drafted or enlisted. The family was very attentive to daily radio news broadcasts that recounted all of the events of the war.

Following the US entering the war, the mobilization of war efforts was quick and effective with car makers and other manufacturers changing to production of weapons of war. Dad used his truck from work to collect and haul scrap in the drives to provide the needed metal for manufacturing those weapons. The US sentiment towards the Japanese following Pearl Harbor showed itself when 120,000 people of Japanese descent were sent to internment camps.

In late 1941/early 1942 the war in the Pacific was not going well with America losing Guam, Hong Kong, Wake, Singapore, and the Philippines, but late that year the US started to turn the war around with major offensives at Midway and The Coral Sea. A new wrinkle in the war effort was including women in their ranks. There were army and coast guard divisions created for women. There were also K-9 units trained and engaged in the war effort for the first time. These additions to the military proved to increase the US's effectiveness in the war effort. My dad's first cousin Parnell married Eleanor, a woman he served with in the military.

The invention in 1942 of a wide, adhesive, water-resistant tape christened "duck tape" by the troops (because water ran off it like water off a duck's back) became widely used by the military. Because of its versatility, it became valuable in many situations, even to the extent that some thought it helped save lives. Although it wasn't initially intended for civilian users, after the war, it was adapted for non-military use and became widespread. The term "duct tape" became more common as it was used most often to wrap and secure ducts.

A movie that was popular, and likely viewed by the Sanford family on complimentary passes in 1942 was *Holiday Inn*. It was known mostly

EARLY MARRIAGE (1933-1943)

for its trademark song "White Christmas" Another movie, likely the most popular with the children, was *Bambi*.

At the outbreak of war, my father was "frozen" to his job as a truck driver. In 1943 he was forced to move his little family from Moorhead to Detroit Lakes as it was at the junction of two US highways. The North/South Road was highway 59 and the East/West highway 10. The family packed up and 222 East Main Street, in Detroit Lakes, Minnesota became home for the next nearly 50 years.

Red River of the North April 1934 flood in Mom and Dad's neighborhood

The Claud Sanford family Dad's Parents, siblings and spouses
Left to Right
Row 1: Hazel, Claud, Jessie and Winnie
Row 2: Mom, Dad, Dick and Pearl Bosteter
Row 3: Alice and Charles Allman, Brother Harry and sister Marion

Christmas 1951

Chapter 4
Move to Detroit Lakes (1943-1952)

This chapter tells the story of raising children and completing her family from the time of their forced midwinter move in 1943 when the needs of the war effort dictated their relocation and continues through 1952 when the last child was born only a few weeks before their oldest, Barbara, left for college. Their new home was not fancy, but it had a nice porch on the south side.

The house at 222 East Main Street was rented and at some point, purchased and was home from that day forward. My father never borrowed money as his family lost their farm east of Ulen to the bank during the depression. Sometime after the war was over and they had made peace with living in Detroit Lakes, instead of returning to Moorhead, the house was purchased for $1800 cash. The average cost of a new house was $4,075.00 which indicated that the house was definitely below average.

With this purchase they inherited three renters, automatically making them landlords. The renters were Grandma Quinlog, Edna Jones, and another unnamed person who was replaced by Dad's cousin soon after the Sanford family purchased the home. Rotating renters came and went in the cast of characters, who, over the years shared the dwelling with our family. Average rent in the 1940's was $32 a month so this generated a significant boost to the family income. It also eliminated the need to outlay the rent themselves.

The house still stands on a nice corner lot on a little knoll about three steps up from the sidewalk and then three porch steps which led to the front door which faced south, the preferred location for protection from the Minnesota north winds. The wraparound porch seemed welcoming and provided a good place to play out of the wind. The front door opened to a steep stairway straight ahead. Off the entrance was a door to the left and a door to the right. Through the left door, there was a larger bedroom and a hallway that led to two smaller bedrooms. The door on the right led to the living room with a picture window which took up the majority of the south wall of the room. The large window had some rectangles of different colors of glass in a panel which took up the top fourth of the window. Through an archway, there was a dining area and a door to the tiny kitchen addition that was a step-down and included just a sink and counter combination, stove, and a leaky old icebox. Toward the back of the house somewhere among the bedrooms, below the upstairs half bath, was the family bathroom which included a toilet stool, tub, and sink.

Across from the bathroom stood the door to the cellar where a huge coal furnace took up the entirety of the cave-like basement. There was a bin that had a shoot opening from the outside where coal or wood funneled into the basement near the furnace. The furnace required attention 24 hours a day during the heating season. There was great skill involved in building a fire, especially one that could last most of the night. The first step to restoring the fire the next morning would be to shake out the clinkers (the stony residue from the burned coal and ash) so that the fire could burn efficiently while the men were gone at work. Furnace duties were the responsibility of our family, mostly Dad unless he had a long day and mom would have to pinch hit–but never the children. The basement with the first floor, was considered Sanford territory.

The stairway that led to the renters' domain was enclosed and was dark with a single bulb suspended. The bulb weakly illuminated the upstairs landing. The landing had a door to the left which opened into a large single room with a ceiling that sloped with the roof line and had a double window facing west. There was a chimney at the peak of the roof. The door to a tiny half bath was slightly to the right of the landing.

The roof sloped in such a way that you needed to use caution when rising from the toilet so as not to bump your head. The small window took up the entire west wall of the bathroom and overlooked the shed roof. There was space for an average-sized person to stand erect only in front of the tiny sink. The smaller-than-normal door opened outward and was secured with a hook and eye when occupied. Straight ahead, as you came out of the bathroom, was a hall that ran parallel to the stairs created by the wall that closed off the stairs on the right as you looked up from the entrance. Opposite the doorway to the half bath at the other end of the hall was a door to a room that had a double window on the south with the roof sloping down to the top of the window. There was a chimney to the left as you entered the room. Another door bisected the hall wall opposite the wall that enclosed the staircase. This door opened into a room with a chimney on the right and a ceiling that sloped down to the left to the top of the single window on the north. This room was the coldest due to the northern exposure and probably rented for a dollar or two less because of this fact. It was also slightly smaller than the room at the end of the hallway sans the approximately 100 square feet used to create the hallway. This layout was convenient to have 3 sets of renters upstairs who shared the bathroom.

There were no heat registers from the furnace in the upstairs rooms. During the winter months, each room had an oil burner hooked up to the chimney in the room. The oil was purchased and carried up by the able-bodied renters. Edna's beau, or sometimes the men in our family, would assist in toting the oil cans to the second floor for any lady renters. There was no water upstairs except in the tiny sink in the shared bathroom. The renters were responsible for making sure the pipe didn't freeze. This task was accomplished by wrapping the pipes with rags for insulation and judiciously managing the balance of using a heating bulb safely to keep the pipe open on the coldest day while avoiding starting the house on fire.

In the summer the stoves were dismantled and stored. Some of the tenants had electric hot plates where they might cook meals, other times, they might bring in items that required no preparation.

Groceries were limited and precious items such as sugar were rationed. Fortunately for the young family, their parents had gardens and canned. The extended family also had livestock which provided eggs, milk, and meat.

The first year was difficult I'm sure for the children starting school midyear. Vance and Eva set about figuring out their new community while still assisting their families of origin.

In 1943 the Pentagon, considered to be the world's largest office building, was completed as well as the Jefferson Memorial. If Dad was anything like he was in later years in following construction projects he could figure out how many truckloads of gravel that were needed for each day's progress.

Rationing was extended in 1943 to more essential items such as shoes, canned food, meat, cheese, butter, and cooking oils. In the past, it was more non-essential such as sugar. It was my understanding that my parents would often share their rations with renters or others who were needier than they were, as they had meat and home-canned items available to them.

Also, in 1943, future President Lt. John F. Kennedy's command, the PT-109, was sunk by a Japanese destroyer. US General Dwight D. Eisenhower became the supreme Allied commander. The planning for *the D-DAY invasion (Operation Overlord) that* started on June 6, 1944, with Allied forces crossing the English Channel to land in Normandy foreshadowed the end of the war in Europe. *1945 major news stories included:*

- USS Indianapolis is sunk by a Japanese Submarine

- War In Europe Ends May 7th (V-E Day)

- Adolf Hitler and his wife of one day, Eva Braun, commit suicide

- Harry S. Truman becomes US President following the death of President Roosevelt

Move to Detroit Lakes (1943-1952)

- Nuclear Bombs dropped on Hiroshima and Nagasaki

- Japan surrenders on August 14 (V-J Day)

- German Concentration Camps Liberated

- Yalta Agreement signed, Germany is divided

- The United Nations Charter creates the United Nations

The exhilaration of the end of the war was palpable. There were celebrations to welcome home the friends and relatives that had served. A few continued in the military as there was nothing to come home to. In the years since they left, parents had died and girlfriends had forgotten them. On a more positive note, some could earn a better living in the military or start a new career made possible through taking advantage of training funded by the GI Bill. With their new skills some chose to make a new start in a more temperate climate and their loved ones came to them.

My mother heralded the news of the creation of the Jewish state of Israel in 1948 with glee. She recognized this as a fulfillment of Bible prophecy.

My mother was not a robust woman. She suffered from debilitating migraine headaches. She likely had many miscarriages during this time and was thrilled to have a nearly full-term pregnancy.

One of the saddest days of this period was May 21, 1950. On that day Eva's son, John Peter, was born and died shortly after birth. My mother wrote a letter to my dad's sister Hazel. The facts contained in the letter were used to create a narrative from my mother's perspective.

Vance, my husband of almost 17 years stood in the doorway of my hospital room. He looked just like Gregory Peck in overalls. His crop of unkept hair had been crushed down like the lawn in our side yard, by his hat, which was now he respectfully held in his hand. He was so busy with work that it seemed to be swallowing him up. They keep piling more work on him. He's up to his eyeballs between his three jobs. Now, with the added hospital bills I am sure he is feeling the weight of the world on his shoulders. Yet his voice, gentle as a dove, floated toward me 'Eva, you have to stay in the hospital until you are completely okay'. He waved goodbye from the doorway and was gone as swiftly as the wind that seemed to carry him toward his truck. He needed to get another load in before sundown; make sure the three teenagers got their supper; get the lawn mowed; be certain that no one needed anything for school tomorrow (the last day of the school year); and when he could finally be alone in our bed, let the flood of tears break the dam of his determination.

Barbara, my eldest, will begin her first day of work at her first job on Monday, Memorial Day, the beginning of tourist season, the busiest time of the year for the 412 lakes area. Shirley (13 years old) and Hubert (12 years old) would be left to their own devices without their elder sister's stabilizing influence. Contemplating the possible repercussions that could ensue as a result of my Irish twins being left on their own was terrifying. Their checkered history, fueled by irresponsible disregard of the laws of nature, and general lack of common sense was exponentially increased when they were together. Previous escapades had resulted in broken bones and property loss. I am saddened knowing that my absence will only exacerbate the situation.

We lost our son John Peter five days ago. It seems like five years. It is still hard for me to believe but it is a small thing compared to what many others suffer. One lady has a big baby and is dry. I'm here I have no baby and all the milk is going to waste. Most go home in four to five days and I'll be here nine, at least, but it is cheaper in the long run than having to come back. I found out that we ought to be especially thankful the situation is over without any more serious consequences. Mrs. Rock, the neighbor we babysit for, was here as she is a nurse who gives anesthesia for certain operations. I am near the operating room so she came in to see me. She gave me the most satisfactory explanation of the deal. She said she can't understand how I could have gone this long as something was radically wrong from the start and doctors have agreed that these cases develop defectively for either both mother and child as affected.

I wasn't allowed to see John Peter. Dr. Rex said it isn't a good policy. I'm so thankful the kids were allowed to see their baby brother as I felt they had some part of it in that way. I had such good company with him and enjoyed the pregnancy so much. I am still rather lost and lonesome but my nerves are improving and the babies crying doesn't tear me apart anymore like it did. I look at them and enjoy them.

My Mom returned home after the extended hospital time. If anyone deserved to have postpartum depression, she did! There are no records or photos from that time that was shrouded in sadness.

The Korean War began in 1950 when North Korea invaded South Korea and the exhilaration of the end of WW II was muted by this new war.

In 1951 *I Love Lucy* premiered on television on the CBS network. The Sanford family members were huge fans from the beginning of the show. My understanding is, anecdotally, that the three teenagers enjoyed dancing to the beat of the new rock and roll music, notwithstanding what I believe was a church prohibition.

In December of 1951, my mother became pregnant again. Due to her multiple pregnancies, and miscarriages, this must have been a particularly sensitive subject for her. And, in those days the news was not generally shared openly as it is today. Women didn't discuss it unless it was asked directly, or until it had become obvious.

One can only imagine the anxiety and chaos of the summer of 1952 while Mom was in her last trimester of pregnancy. Not to mention that these days were also leading up to their first child leaving home. Life was hectic. Barbara, Shirley, and Hubert did shift work into the late-night hours at the A & W drive-in. This left little time for the preparations that needed to be made for Barbara to go to an unfamiliar place for college. The raising of the three oldest children was nearly complete.

Sylvia's Dedication, December 1952

Chapter 5
Launching of the Older Offspring (1952-1962)

In 1952, Elizabeth II became Queen of England and the Sanford family launching years began shortly after my birth when my sister, the oldest child, Barbara, left for college. This chapter gets at some of the issues of the first child leaving the nest at the same time the nest got a new occupant.

The tiny Church of the Nazarene which Eva Sanford attended with her children in tow did not have much pomp and ceremony. There was only the occasional mid-summer baptism service at a nearby lake and communion at the stroke of midnight at the watch night service. Since the denomination's statement of beliefs did not allow for infant baptism but rather a believer's baptism, babies were dedicated. The parents stood before the assembly and the pastor solicited a response from the parents that they intended to raise this child in the "nurture and admonition of the Lord". To the casual observer, dedication day looked a lot like infant baptism as the pastor usually tapped the baby on the head with a rose that had been dipped in water.

The photo focuses on a dozen people who attended the obligatory post-dedication meal. The front window in the living room, with a view of Main Street, was the usual backdrop for indoor photos. The shade which was primarily designed to eliminate the prying eyes of those passing by doubled as prevention of every photographer's nightmare, backlighting. The attendees were grouped around the happy parents,

Eva and Vance, or "Daddy" Sanford. Daddy was seated cradling me and Mom was at his left. Eva was dressed in a dark dress with her beautiful, wavy raven hair clipped back and a hint of knee showing at the bottom of the frame. She was leaning into Vance with her cheek softly touching his left shoulder. She had a gentle smile and her right arm was encircling her husband of almost 20 years. Dad was in a crisp starched and pressed white shirt and tie, very uncharacteristic considering his usual uniform was a pair of dirty bib overalls. Daddy had a straight-line mouth, which seemed to indicate his discomfort. There were lots of reasons to be uncomfortable today for a common man who generally avoided the spotlight. Being a 48-year-old man with a four-month-old was in itself remarkable, and perhaps a little embarrassing by Minnesota standards. The expression might also have resulted from repressing his urge to fight the scratchy tightness of the unfamiliar collar which he had been strongly entreated by his loving wife to wear to church. In addition to the shirt and tie attire requirement he had spent all morning in one of his least favorite places and he was likely getting hungry. Church was an awkward place for him as the roll-your-own cigarettes he created and enjoyed were forbidden. Smoking was a sin as far as the Nazarenes were concerned. The combination of no nicotine and looks of disapproval for showing up on this special day when he was usually absent could make one uncomfortable. This in addition to sitting still for far too long made church attendance excruciating. Since Dad had never visited a dentist in his life, his straight-line mouth also served to conceal his sparse brown teeth which was a part of the propriety needed for the special photo. He usually, unselfconsciously, flashed his snaggle-toothed grin to one and all freely, but not today.

I was in a christening dress, handmade for the occasion by the mother of my oldest sister Barbara's best friend, Geneva. Eva did not sew except to patch the everyday clothes or make simple items such as pillow covers which she used to change the décor when she would find an appropriate quantity of fabric, which she liked at the Salvation Army thrift store or a rummage sale. Most everything that the family put on their backs was the product of Eva's relentless searches at rummage sales. The creation of the gown for the baby was expected of the mother but with her usual aplomb, she accepted this kind gift from her friend without any shame. I was not looking toward the camera so there was only a profile view of me, who was supposed to be the central figure. Daddy was the usual photographer and I was probably unsure of where to look. The identity of the photographer is an enigma.

Flanking the central trio on the right was Casey, my 19-year-old sister Barbara's boyfriend. Casey, who had likely just arrived home on leave from Korea, was proudly dressed in his military uniform. Barbara was on her first visit home from college for the event. She had probably traveled almost 1,300 miles through the mountains in December in the last few days arriving just in time for the festivities. Barbara was standing behind Casey with her hands placed properly on his shoulders. Her expression mirrored her father's, perhaps because she was thinking she needed to break up with Casey before making the return journey to the college life she had learned to love in these few short months. She was determined to return and avoid the matrimonial intentions of her soldier.

Next to Mom on the left was Charlie, sister Shirl's new, much older boyfriend. He worked for the highway department and Daddy had introduced the pair. His untanned forehead and area around his eyes peered out of his plaid shirt testifying to his hard outdoor work and lack of fashion sense. The absence of Charlie's smile may have indicated he was uncomfortable being present at this auspicious occasion when they had just started dating. Shirley, my 16-year-old sister, sat on a stool behind Charlie sort of sidesaddle. Shirley was beaming and although it was out of the camera frame, her left arm seemed to have his left shoulder locked in a solid side hug.

There are four unidentified females of various ages jumbled in the middle completing the second row and forcing one member into the third row. The other person in the third row is my 15-year-old brother Hubert or "Sonny" as most people call him. His mischievous smile was peeking out between Barbara and one of the mystery women. He appeared to be standing on his tip toes and a little off balance to be as tall as his big sister, Barb. The expression on Sister Barb's face may have also indicated the fact that she had been on her own for four months and was a little irritated with her younger brother's shenanigans.

In telling the story of the launching of the children there are two concerns that I have. The first concern is that I did want to be respectful particularly to sacred things. Please keep in mind that any of the personal embellishments I made to add to the story should be viewed in the context of kindness and respect and no offense is intended. Since there are no diaries from 1952 -1963, I assumed that the people, places, and things mentioned in the diaries my mother kept in later years of this period were similar. The second concern is that I may not have been as objective as I read and interpreted the diary entries but filtered them through my eleven to seventeen-year-old eyes as the events were part of my memory.

Barbara was the first to set out on her own when she went to Northwest Nazarene College (N.N.C.) in Nampa, Idaho. N.N.C. was the designated college where funds from the churches in the educational region helped to mitigate the hefty tuition. Barbara was a diligent student and I'm sure received some scholarships. She also worked as a waitress and some hours at the public library while in high school from the time that she was 16. She continued her employment at the library and waitressing when she came home from college in the summer. The college librarian, a Minnesota girl herself and acquainted with my mom, put Barb right to work and let her work as many hours as she could around her studies.

Barb was introduced to Art Manchester while she was a student at N.N.C. They may have had one official date while in school or Art might just have served as Barb's escort to a college event for education majors. But Barbara became engaged to another man before any relationship with Art developed. That engagement was broken off and when she graduated from N.N.C. in May 1956 she was unattached. That fall she began teaching junior high English and Social Studies in Stewartville, Minnesota, almost three hundred miles away from home. Barbara held this position for several years.

LAUNCHING OF THE OLDER OFFSPRING (1952-1962)

Barbara had come to love showering when she was in college. She made sure her apartment had a shower and she longed to be able to shower on her visits home. So, in 1957 when Barbara finished her first year of teaching, she paid to have the bathroom in her parent's home renovated, including installing a tub-shower combination. The pipes froze the first winter so the tub was only connected in the warm months and we went back to the old way of washing with a basin "spit baths" as my mother called them, during the winter. The old tub had been directly above the furnace and not used much in the winter, so the pipe freezing had not been an issue. The long shower pipe tipped the balance in favor of the relentless Minnesota cold.

Barbara was able to travel during her summer vacations from school and made a trip to Europe, which made her mother very proud. One of her stops was to see her old neighbor Yvonne Kohler, who had fled back to France when her marriage to an American soldier failed. There were many wonderful days of travel and reconnecting in person with Yvonne and her family.

After several years Barbara moved to teach the same subjects in Benson, Minnesota, a bit closer to home, only a little over a hundred miles from Detroit Lakes. Barbara was now close enough to come home for visits more often and for her parents and young sister Sylvia to come for special events including the plays that she directed.

Sometime in the fall of 1960, Barb received a letter from Art Manchester. Never being one to dive into anything without due consideration she did not respond. Approximately a year later Barb received another letter from her persistent suitor, Art Manchester, this time with a photo enclosed. The details of the long-distance courtship are not clear but likely there was a visit home at Christmas 1961 to meet the folks and Barb visited Portland to see Art over spring break when they became engaged. Barbara married Art Manchester on Friday, August 10, 1962. It was a beautiful wedding with the bridesmaids dressed in Barbara's favorite color green and I was in the center of all the activity at the local Baptist church in Detroit Lakes surrounded by familiar faces. I also enjoyed being a part of all the planning and festivities to prepare for the wedding.

Barbara had a rehearsal dinner at a local restaurant, a fancy event the likes of which I had never been involved with before and I had a seat of honor next to my beloved sister. In our rural area of Minnesota wedding gowns were often handed down, or, the mother of the bride (or the bride herself) would make the dress. Lacking an heirloom gown, and since neither Barb nor Mom were accomplished seamstresses, Barb rented hers. Although she had a strong fashion sense and expensive taste, she also had a practical side which kept her from feeling comfortable in making such a costly purchase for one-time use. Renting her dress, since it didn't have to be transported back to Portland, Oregon – a more than 1500-mile trek - also helped free up space in the tiny Ford Falcon for all the belongings required to set up housekeeping for the young couple. My brother returned the dress to the exclusive Minneapolis shop after the wedding and the magic was over. After the wedding, the couple spent their honeymoon driving back to Oregon where they set up housekeeping together in a small rented house shortly before they started teaching.

That fall was difficult as there were no trips to Benson for plays or visits from Barb. The idea of the wedding was great but the reality of the separation took hold especially when Barbara was not there to celebrate my tenth birthday.

The next child to launch was Shirley when she graduated from high school in 1954 and attended N.N.C. for one year where she was her sister's roommate. Shirley then transferred to the Methodist Kahler School of Nursing, in Rochester, Minnesota, a school associated with the hospital where many physicians from the Mayo Clinic practiced medicine. The transfer was necessary as the nursing program at N.N.C. did not fully develop. During nursing school and her early employment, Shirley brought friends home for holiday breaks. One of those friends, Marilyn Kirgess, taught me to ride a bicycle on one of those visits. After finishing nurses' training the highlight of her early nursing career was being the head scrub nurse during open heart surgery for the esteemed Dr. John Kirkland at the Mayo Clinic. I do remember thinking that I didn't want to be a nurse as I never saw Shirley after she started working.

Several years later Shirley returned to Nampa, Idaho, with two other registered nurses – they roomed together but did not work together. Two roommates worked at Mercy Hospital. Shirley had a position at Samaritan Hospital which is where she met her future husband, Randolph Howard Metcalfe ("Howard"), who also worked at Samaritan.

The outstanding memory that I have is that Howard bought me a stunning China tea set with service for four. I had never received such a wonderful gift so beautifully wrapped. I was taken up with my sister Barbara in our usual interaction as it had been for every Christmas I could remember. I had a twinge of jealousy about Art being there in our family time. It struck me that I barely knew my sister Shirley.

Howard was always fond of his car. When they met, he had a blue Ford Fairlane and they used to go for drives usually to see gladiolas growing throughout the countryside. The relationship blossomed and they married on December 15, 1962, in Nampa, Idaho. Hubert, very efficient in his travel facilitation role, bought a roadworthy car and drove Mom, Grandma Larsen, and me through the mountains in December for the nuptials, as airline service was not that good to this Idaho outpost. I was a candlelighter at the wedding. Sister Barbara was there and served as matron of honor. I remember my joy to see Barbara as it was the longest separation in my memory and felt shy among all the people that I did not know in the big strange church. I nearly muffed my candlelighter duties. The reception was weird as the wedding cake was fruit cake covered with frosting, thanks to Howard's Canadian heritage. A Canadian tradition, I guess. I felt cheated that I had not been in on the planning and my heart broke when Barb and Art left and we started the arduous journey home.

Howard and Shirley's honeymoon was a road trip to their first home in Oklahoma where Howard finished his studies at Bethany Nazarene College obtaining a degree in Education. They both worked at Saint

Anthony's Hospital where Shirley worked in surgery and Howard worked in administration.

Hubert went to the University of Minnesota in the fall of 1955. The Minnesota Department of Rehabilitation Services paid his tuition and expenses in full. Early in 1953, he suffered an injury caused by the typing room's round metal door handle hitting him directly in the hip joint, shattering it, as he walked down the hall after class dismissal. He was in bed for one year in a cast. At that time, I, his baby sister, fell hopelessly in love with him as I reportedly spent many contented hours propped up against his cast with his full attention. The Christmas/dedication photo at the beginning of this chapter was the last with him standing before the accident. The living room where the photo had been taken, was transformed into "Hub's hospital" as several referred to it with a wry smile. Through home study with his mother as his teacher, he was able to complete high school on time. His leg did not grow after that and he went through the rest of his life wearing a built-up shoe. His college career was short-lived, perhaps one semester. He got a job at Northwest Airlines and spent his entire work life there until his retirement. He also flipped houses using his carpenter skills. He continued the family tradition of using his home as a rental for an extra source of income. In his case, his renters were not little old ladies but men who would assist in his various projects and did not mind living in a construction zone.

Art and Barbara Manchester, August 10, 1962 | Howard and Shirley Metcalfe, December 15, 1962

The loves of Hubert's life houses and cars

Mom's "kids and grandkids", August 1972

Chapter 6
Just Three at Home (1963-1970)

There are no diary entries to confirm many of the years of my mom's home life. Life was, I'm sure, very different for my older three siblings than it was for me, but the things that were the same were the love, provision for, and concern for family and friends in a way that could be called radical. I will start with the earliest memories that I have of our home life as I knew it in the fall of 1957.

True to form as a trailblazing trendsetter, my mother enrolled me in the first kindergarten class in Detroit Lakes. She was criticized for this decision by many. There was only one class at the Rossman School, on the south end, where the rich, progressive, professional people made their homes. No one else in our neighborhood went and I was the only one who boarded the bus at Washington School, the farthest north point of the route. Most of the students walked the few short blocks from their well-appointed homes, however, we did pick up some children who were initially strangers. But, during that year I came to know them and became fast friends with the other nineteen students in what I found to be a magical year.

Our teacher had special training in kindergarten teaching, per my mom's research. The well-equipped classroom in the new school had toys and games the likes of which I had never had the privilege of previously enjoying. Sometimes Mom would ride the bus and volunteer in the classroom. It was a year of sheer joy filled with learning and new experiences.

My first through sixth grade years were at the Washington Elementary School where my older siblings had attended years before and my sister Barbara and I would swap stories about school on our visits together. There were few shared teachers unless they were very old as the tradition was still to retire when you had a family of your own so only those that were "old maids" or those who returned after their families were raised might have been common to both of us. The only men at the school were the principal and the custodian.

I do not have many recollections of my first through fourth grades but fifth grade was memorable as leading up to the Cuban missile crisis we had drills in school where we hid under our desks. Even as a fifth grader I questioned the effectiveness of these maneuvers. Friends at the nearby Holy Rosary Catholic School would tell stories of being crouched under their desks and praying the Rosary adding a particular layer of protection. Being the woman of faith that she was, my mom recommended that I too, should pray and "Put on the full armor of God".

In my sixth-grade classroom we received the news that John F. Kennedy had been assassinated. It was a heavy blow for our whole community which was largely Catholic Democrats. Sixth grade was the new finale to attendance at Washington school.

The elementary school had included eight grades in the days of my siblings' attendance and some students ended their educational endeavors at that point. All my siblings went to the same high school (grades nine through twelve) as my mother had attended. The seventh and eighth grades had been relocated to the old high school building which had become the Holmes Junior High. Students from three elementary schools joined in there. The distance was still walkable and the train station which was only about four blocks away was a good respite from the wind and cold at the halfway point. I was reunited with some of my kindergarten friends at the junior high.

Some of the outlying communities still maintained the elementary schools with eight grades and so there were new students who came

Just Three at Home (1963-1970)

into the high school from these communities as well as the students that attended the Catholic grade school that went through grade 8. There was a brand-new high school which I was lucky to attend but did usually require some form of transportation. It was over a mile away and not a pedestrian-friendly walk. A few times I needed to walk and performed the death-defying act of crossing US highway 10 four lanes of high-speed traffic. Sometimes, my friend Patty Olson's boyfriend, and now husband, Bob Sanaker, would pick us up for a ride or there was the option of taking the bus from Washington School. After Bob graduated the neighbor across the street usually provided transportation. Mom always encouraged all school activities and I was active in speech contests in junior high and debate in high school. The most memorable event during my high school years occurred during my junior year: the assassination of Martin Luther King Jr. My mother was much more impacted than most. We watched all the activities surrounding his assassination. The average Minnesotan viewed themselves as far-removed from this issue because Minnesota had never been a slave state and it was not on our doorstep.

In our household, getting your driver's license was an important event. Dad was in charge since Mom never drove. Daddy was a man of great patience and he taught all the "Sanford kids" to drive, and a number of our friends whose parents lacked the nerve. He believed that the ability to drive a stick shift car was a necessary skill. Indeed, this skill has served me well through the years. Sadly, the diary recorded that I failed my driving test on the first attempt. The cars that we drove were often old and in disrepair. One of the ways of coping was to avoid coming to a complete stop at stop signs in order to make sure the car did not die. The examiner took a dim view of this practice. We borrowed a car which did not require that kind of illegal maneuvering and I passed my test on the 2nd attempt.

Dad's health was declining due to emphysema caused by his life-long smoking. His ability to do the hard physical work in an unforgiving climate was waning. His job became more uncertain due to a big transition in the trucking industry experienced when the Saint Lawrence

Seaway was opened in 1959. The seaway, a deep draft inland navigation system, the longest in the world, allowed ocean going vessels to travel back and forth the 2,300 miles from the Atlantic Ocean into the North American heartland. Duluth, Minnesota, on the opposite side of the state from Detroit Lakes, became one of the most important inland ports. The ability put iron ore and steel products on a ship was a boon to the Minnesota economy. The growth of the maritime industry in the Duluth area allowed for jobs for areas that had previously been depressed. The trucking industry in Western Minnesota was impacted negatively. The usual rail and over-the-road routes that the Detroit Lakes area was most dependent on, were now more expensive and hence, less popular.

My father was very frugal so as income shrank, he rose to the challenge happily. For example, he traced his foot in the thin cardboard from cereal boxes to cut out several layers as insoles in his shoes, which had holes in the bottom. He would then wear a bread bag over his socks as waterproofing.

Daddy had a fascination for technology that exceeded his frugality and he found the time to look for and money to purchase a good television set. Mom recorded incidences where many friends and neighbors joined us for the parades as it is likely that we had a good color television early on.

The entries in my mother's diary from 1964 to 1969 recounting the January events all included watching the Rose Parade broadcasted on NBC. There were only three channels available. In 1968 watching the Orange Bowl Parade on ABC was added.

There were no church friends there, however, as they were well aware of the evil that television brought "right into your living room!" We sometimes had more than one TV, hence the Orange Bowl addition I presume. There might have been a third added at some point when the Cotton Bowl was included in 1969 on CBS for the first time. Dad was friends with the local appliance store owner and I'm sure bartered hauling items in his truck in return for the televisions originally and subsequently, for the parts he needed to keep things going. He was also

Just Three at Home (1963-1970)

a master of the antenna. Antenna skills were so important in getting the best reception. Watching Daddy's maneuvers to get the perfect picture was almost as much fun as watching the parades.

Many mundane activities were recounted in the diary entries. A big one in the official winter months, January, February and March, was hauling coal or getting wood for the voracious furnaces. Usually, these activities were done with several people. The pastors who had the misfortune of being assigned to our tiny church were often ill equipped for life in the northlands. There was perhaps some personal or ministry failure that led them to Detroit Lakes but it was a topic that was taboo, basically the same protocol as you don't ask someone in prison "what are you in for?" My daddy, prompted by my mother I'm sure, would go out with the pastors to help them learn necessary survival skills such as how to find, cut and haul wood.

The diaries chronicled activities of daily living with washing hair, getting a haircut, shopping or fixing things. Grand news was included as well, like a foreshadowing of my launch with the engagement announcement of my church friend Etta Duke, to one of the boys that rented a room in the Pastor Taylor's basement.

There was always something broken it seemed. It could have been that it was broken before we owned it as it was bought used or Daddy hauled it away, supposedly to the dump. Many of those items took up residence in the two sheds on our property. The sheds were ramshackled but were able to remain upright due to all the things stuffed inside helping the buildings to maintain their shape. A diary entry on January 3rd said that my dad was working on a car. I'm sure there was no place to work on it inside so I'm thinking that's a pretty difficult job to do in the middle of the winter. That would also explain the various car parts that would be splayed out to thaw on the kitchen table for the duration of these repair projects.

My mother had no washing machine except a configuration including an open machine with an electric agitator followed by three rinse tubs. The clothes would be washed clean first, similar to the bath arrangement. After agitation the clothes would be put through a wringer into the first rinse tub. The wringer was able to be swung around and after the clothes were stirred to hand rinse in the first tub, they would be wrung into the second tub for rinsing and lastly through the wringer into the third tub for the final rinse. The clothes were then wrung into a basket to be hung to dry. This process, again much like bathing, was for the months from late spring through early fall. In the summer rainwater would be collected and used for washing clothes. In the winter it would be handwashing and wringing and drying on lines strung throughout the house or outside on the clothes line if the snow wasn't too deep. The clothes would freeze solid and the ice would be knocked off before they were brought in, literally freeze dried. In around 1960 my sister bought Mother an automatic dryer so sometimes she would go to a friend's home who had an automatic washer and bring the clean clothes home to dry.

The one advantage of winter laundry processing is that ironing is not as difficult. The hand wringing did not create the much more resilient wrinkles caused by the mechanical wringer. There were no steam irons at that time so the clothes were ironed before they had completely dried or were sprinkled first. Doing laundry was always preceded by copious warnings about getting your hand caught in the wringer. It was a delicate balance to get the wringer to catch the fabric that needed wringing and not lose an appendage in the process. One time Mom mentioned that a neighbor with a large bosom had a kerfuffle with the wringer. Mom never elaborated but the story certainly managed to strike fear and deter carelessness. The wringer could be hard on clothes as well so buttons needed to be folded in to avoid breakage from the pressure of the wringer. There were people in our circle of acquaintance who were disabled due to a wringer injury.

Ironing could also be dangerous, or so I was often told. Avoiding burns and the possibility of tripping on the cord and burning down the house also needed to be considered. The safety speech concerning ironing was year-round even when the wringer wasn't lurking in the kitchen to maim us. With all the everyday household dangers that surrounded us, it is a wonder that any of us survived.

Just Three at Home (1963-1970)

Winter weather merited frequent diary entries. Weather was described as blowing, snowy, stormy and just plain bad in a number of the nearly 600 official winter days chronicled from 1964-1970. Minnesota winters were often known to break the boundaries of the calendar. Winter might decide to come early as evidenced by the October the 16, 1969, entry was "a snowy stormy day". Sometimes winter stayed on longer. On April 27, 1964, there was ...you guessed it... a blizzard. Yikes! There was a record-breaking low temperature of 42 below zero in 1967 on January 17th. The previous record was set in 1887. That day's diary entry also stated my father worked hauling snow from 6:00 a.m. to 9:00 p.m. as a 60-year-old man. Several times my mother wrote in her diary "I almost froze my face off!"

Ice skating and sledding were the popular outdoor recreational activities. Almost everyone owned a pair of skates that could be adapted with socks and laces so one size fit many, if not well, at least long enough to support the few minutes you could skate outside in the consistently subzero temperatures. The blades could be sharpened easily and even the poorest among us had the equipment needed to have a great time on the ice. We had a neighborhood rink and warming house about three blocks down. Another skating venue could be a pond or nearby lake when friends would shovel off the snow to create a rink for us to enjoy during our visits. A bonfire would be kindled to keep warm.

When it came to sledding a very few owned actual well-crafted, aerodynamic and impressive sleds and toboggans. If you were smart you cultivated a relationship with these folks so you could be a passenger and ride in style. Generally, we sledded on cardboard, or a shovel a la the opening scene in the 1947 film, *It's a Wonderful Life*. A reasonable facsimile of a sled was sometimes fashioned from whatever was at hand. Daddy might have found an actual sled that had seen better days and rescued it from the dump. If there was new fresh snow sledding on the many hills around was unmatched for excitement. Dodging the trees required steering prowess with no actual steering mechanism. Steering was accomplished through a coordinated rendition of body maneuvers akin to Olympic level gymnastics. One Christmas when I was too young to join the group, the Larsen cousins took the hood off one of the old cars in the boneyard of old machinery used for parts. The hood made a marvelous sled for six. Grandpa was not pleased and it resulted in a strict ban on sledding in subsequent family times at the farm.

Quiet family indoor activities were mentioned when the weather was too bad for visiting. One year it was noted that we mounted a farm puzzle that I had completed – another sign of frugality and hoarding. Rather than taking it apart and allowing someone else to enjoy it we added multiple mounted puzzles to the walls of our home or stacked them in storage.

The TV was always the central focus and after the three older children left home, those of us still living in the house ate most meals on TV trays. After all, we needed the kitchen table for car parts and other projects.

On many days my mother made note of food consumed or prepared. A few of the items she mentioned were boiled raisin bars, various kinds of pie (pumpkin was the star but apple, cherry, peach, blueberry and rhubarb received honorable mention), date bars, date bread, date cake, corn bread, banana bread, jelly roll, rhubarb cake, plain old sourdough or yeast bread, cinnamon rolls, biscuits and chicken and dumplings. The only entrée mentioned was chicken and dumplings and this dish was very central to our existence. It was a shock when I moved to Illinois and what they called dumplings were thick gummy noodles, nothing like the delicious light creations of my youth.

Holiday menus always included turkey, lefse (traditional Norwegian potato flatbread), and pumpkin pie. Pumpkin pie was on the regular menu as it was my brother Hubert's favorite so if Mom were making a pumpkin pie outside of holiday time that usually meant Hugh was coming from "the cities" for a visit. Donuts and dumplings were simple and cheap and would be offered to unexpected guests. Eating out was not a luxury we enjoyed and we either packed a lunch or ate with friends or family if we would be away from home at mealtime. Whoever came in the door at breakfast, lunch, or suppertime shared whatever was the fare of the day. The list of what was baked or cooked likely was based on what was in season or on sale. Rutabaga soup was my least favorite whether at home or elsewhere. One year there was a bumper crop of rutabagas and the seemingly endless number of meals of the soup cemented my resolve to never eat another rutabaga the rest of my life. Our family received government surplus commodities of peanut butter, cheese and some canned meats at times so these items were incorporated into the meals to save on more expensive items. Since there was no real guarantee that you would have all items needed for a specific recipe cooking was more a spontaneous exercise of putting together a meal using staples and whatever else you had on hand. A common source of contention between my parents was getting groceries since Mom didn't drive. Dad worked long hours so she would sometimes walk to the store and carry home what she could. It was problematic when dad got groceries because he did not follow the list. Her diary read "Vance got groceries which means he bought whatever was on sale and then I am supposed to figure out what to do with it!"

Ever since 1957 when the space race started with Russia's Sputnik I and the United States responded with creation of the National Aeronautics and Space Administration in 1958, we avidly followed all space news and broadcasts. When it came to space-related viewing opportunities the church folks would make an exception to enjoying television viewing with us. On March 13, 1969, several from the congregation were present for watching the Apollo 9 splashdown. In Mom's usual concise fashion, she recorded this as "watched astronauts".

May was the month when cleaning became a priority to get rid of the evidences of the wood and coal fires that burned for most of the last six months. It was a time of putting away the winter clothes and airing out. May 23, 1965 provided an unwelcome surprise when my mother noted, "cold–went back to winter clothes". Every year in the diary years, and I presume in the undocumented years before, there was attendance at a Memorial Day parade and visits to the cemetery to decorate the family graves.

Other activities noted in the diary during the month of June included more cleaning out the house particularly when the May weather had not cooperated. Quilts were aired and furniture was moved to the upstairs room. In June 1964 Bernice Larsen came to rent a room at our house. Bernice was the ex-wife of Grandpa Larsen's brother, Jim. My mother had a soft spot for Bernice as I think she pitied her for putting up with a life in a shack with a dirt floor and no conveniences where she raised four children. She finally left the marriage when the children were grown and was now nearing retirement age and had health problems exacerbated by years of menial labor she had been engaged in to make ends meet. Mom helped her apply for Social Security. I remember Mom working with her on many business-related tasks during the time she rented from us. Another renter, Hank, was mentioned. Mom cleaned his room, since it was likely not expected of a man to do his own cleaning. I would sometimes help.

A new in-home purchasing opportunity was mentioned in 1964 for the first time, the Jewel Tea man. I remember that the gentleman was a teacher doing this as a summer job. Mom ordered melamine dishes. She had been fascinated with this new phenomenal product ever since my sisters had received some melamine pieces as wedding gifts. There were the usual Tupperware and Stanley parties as well as visits from the Avon lady.

The hallmark of spring's arrival in late May or early June was when Dad borrowed a trailer and loaded the back yard junk or things that had become junk after being covered by snow for many months. He was then able to mow after work during the long evening hours. My usual part of the spring sprucing up process was to buy more petunias to go with the one my mom received on Mother's Day and plant them as my Mother's Day tribute whenever the weather allowed.

My mom penned an entry in her diary that I bought a tie for my boyfriend, Lowell. Also mentioned was that Lowell's brother, Bob Schlauderaff, bought a new Oldsmobile. Perhaps the tie was to wear on an occasion to celebrate the new ride, but although the statements were juxtaposed there was no indication about the why of either, or if they were actually connected in a real way.

Just Three at Home (1963-1970)

If someone purchased a new home, new refrigerator, a new stove, or a new anything we would make a visit in order to admire the acquisition. The protocol varied depending on what was purchased. If it were a stove or refrigerator, it would be all the women gathering in the kitchen. The men were excluded except for perhaps a comment regarding that the cookies they were served were made in the new oven or the cold drinks had ice from the beautiful frost-free freezer. Another item of home visiting decorum was to mention and ask to take a closer look at the cards displayed for whatever recent occasion. Your comments needed to be not too profuse but understated and sincere, Minnesota style.

Often the summer weather was described as dark and stormy. A trip to Fargo to view straw that had been driven through a telephone post by the tornado came alive from my memory. Surveying the damage in a nearby town had both practical applications as well as just part of being nosey.

June seemed to be the time for defrosting the refrigerator. There was no automatic defrost and it would take hours to let the ice melt. Despite aggressive chiseling with an icepick and using pans of heated water to encourage melting with pans and rags in strategic locations attempting to capture the run off to hasten the chore it was still a nearly an all-day process. The timing was critical as the food needing refrigeration had to be at a minimum. There was an effort made to consume the contents of the refrigerator before starting as well as preparing something that would keep for lunch on defrost day. Any small amount that needed to be held over was placed in the sink covered with old clean rag rugs with the chipped-away ice placed under the rug around the food. Sometimes someone who rented locker space at a nearby meat processing facility would allow us to use some of their spot during that day. Every inch of the refrigerator was sorely needed in the summer so defrosting was imperative to create space and avoid food spoilage. Winter was easier as the whole of the great outdoors was safe food storage in terms of temperature. The containers did need to be secured in a manner to discourage the animals that roved about.

Detroit Lakes was a big baseball town and going to the American Legion games was possibly a holdover from when my sisters' boyfriends played. Now the occasional cousin, nephew or friend needed spectators and we would rally to the cause for support.

One of the highlights of the summer was the county fair in which the diary mentioned that I had several entries. Fair attendance by the church folks was limited to the barns and other display buildings not associated with the carnival.

Health was a theme of the diaries throughout the years. The headaches that had plagued Mom in earlier years thankfully seemed to disappear with menopause. Mom made comments like "today I had the blurs". I assume she had vision problems related to her high blood pressure. There were many references to feeling tired or "punk". There was only one mention of ever going to a medical doctor because medication was needed. The chiropractor, Dr. Wething, was in truth my mother's primary health care provider. Many diary notations indicated that she had gone to Dr. Wething for feeling punk, dizzy, tired, ... Of particular interest to me was her entry that she had gone to see Dr. Wething for "the itch".

The Western Minnesota Steam Thresher's Reunion held annually in Rolag, Minnesota was the crowning event of the summer and has been held on Labor Day weekend every year since 1954. The property near the tiny town about 25 miles from our home became a busy city with a post office, newspaper with a steam press, theater, steam train, churches, restaurants and stores, all reminiscent of the late 19th century. People from around the world brought their restored equipment to display and compete. There was all manner of steam equipment from tiny operational models only a few inches long to giants with wheels twice the height of the tallest man in attendance. The pinnacle of the event was live threshing demonstrations and competitions. The fall was the time to begin school again, concentrate on harvest and preparation for the onslaught of winter.

The H.F. Larsen family

Chapter 7
Cast of Characters

The family and friends that Mom entertained in our home came in all shapes and sizes. The names of individuals listed in the diary ranged from some with a one-time listing with no explanation such as "Vi dropped by" other names were repeated almost daily in multiple contexts. Some were strict churchgoers and others never darkened the doorway of a church. Regardless of how you might try to describe Mom's guests they typically fell into three categories: Category One–the poor and needy who would never be able to return her hospitality; Category Two–those who worked together on a personal or church project and shared a simple meal that was practical and brief to support the task getting done; finally, Category Three–official church royalty such as the pastor, visiting preachers, church officials or missionaries or non-church royalty such as anyone visiting from out of state, local, county or state officials or officers in organizations that Mom belonged to. Her hospitality also extended outside of our home to those who attended family dinners or dinners hosted at the church or other organizations. Mom enthusiastically participated. She always brought more than her share. Her dishes were always displayed with lovely presentation on beautiful China or unusual trays she had gathered in her thrift store shopping, seeing in her mind's eye the beauty that the piece would add to a bountiful table at any occasion.

Family First

The three Larsen sisters were always close. Evelyn worked outside the home all of her life selling sewing machines and was very active politically. Her oldest son Jerry was close to my brother's age and Joanne, Redtop, Carrot Top, or Joanie as my dad most often referred to her affectionately, was 5 years younger. One day when Joanne came home from high school and needed to get ready for work her mom chided her that an important visitor, Muriel Humphrey, wife of Senator Hubert Humphrey, and the current democratic candidate for POTUS, was taking a nap in Joanne's room and her mom indicated firmly "you will just need to be a little late for work today".

Jerry and any boys that went out to the Larsen farm had a great time and pitched in with the work. Joanne and any other girls could easily die of boredom or fright. If it happened to be a Saturday the guests must have endured the dreaded lifebuoy scrub. On any other night, the only thing to contend with were the bats that flew in and around the upstairs. In the morning Grandma would take down the bats that had gotten entangled in the sheer curtains, methodically wrap them in paper, and conduct cremations using the kitchen stove. Evidently bats were not a protected species at that time or Grandma didn't know or care to find out.

Evelyn was very prissy and fashion-conscious and dressed elegantly with beautiful jewelry and had her nails and hair done to perfection. Joanne was more of a tomboy and preferred simple dress. She was not allowed to wear jeans at home but my mom had a pair for her that she would gleefully wear whenever she visited and it was their secret.

Mayme was busy with her brood and always lived in Warren, about 100 miles away so it was not as easy to keep the ties as close during those hectic years.

Parallel launching of the Larsen cousins was occurring in the extended family. Jerry was the first of the Larsen cousins to get married on June 18, 1960, and he and his wife settled into a basement apartment in the Moorhead area. Evelyn was the first to be a grandmother when Todd joined the family on May 4, 1961. His brother Tim joined the family not quite two years later on April 25, 1963. The couple desired to have a daughter and Heidi, born on November 1, 1968, was adopted into the family. Jerry had health problems related to suffering from juvenile diabetes. Beverly was mainly a stay-at-home mom.

Joanne married Lynn Ward on June 3, 1967. Their first-born Paul was welcomed into the family on January 18, 1969. Their family was completed almost three years later when baby Patrick was born. The Ward family although by all accounts 100% Norwegian on the Ward side and 50% Norwegian on the Olmsted side might have had some gypsy ancestry. They moved around a lot, having as many as 40 residences, if you count their five years in a 5th wheel.

There are many references to visiting Mama. Interestingly, Grandpa was usually not mentioned as Grandma Larsen ruled the roost. My mother's mother, Grandma Larsen, was widowed after 50 years of marriage. She lived alone in their country home with no indoor plumbing until she fell and broke her hip. She lived with us for a short time but the situation was untenable for several reasons. She then became a resident of Emmanuel Nursing Center. A letter I recently received from my cousin Donna Jordahl, avid family historian, shed some light on the situation. This letter from my mother was dated Thursday, December 17, 1964, and was addressed to Donna's parents, Rena and Claude Robbins:

"November 13th Mama moved from here to Emmanual Nursing Home right here in town a fabulous million-dollar place which she likes & is happy at. I was out to see her today with some mail & extra things for her to wear. I am rather the trouble shooter as I am the only child living here and my sisters both work one in Moorhead & one in Warren. Right after July 4th Mama began to have serious trouble with her right leg which was diagnosed as infection of the blood vein on the outside of the right leg. The leg seemed to explode into deep crevices which really are ulcers draining and healing-The Lord wonderfully answered prayer & the infection halted before amputation of the leg became necessary. The suffering was tremendous but she fought it out and now is getting around with a cane. Mama was in bed from (July) 6th to November 5th first time up & dressed. It was a wheelchair first a walker and now only a cane. There is plenty of pain in the right leg and swelling in both limbs as she is ambitious to get around & visit.... Did I make it clear that Mama became sick and was here the whole time from about July 15 to Nov 13 Drs didn't think she needed to be hospitalized at any time so here we were in 3 rooms. My feet & legs became troublesome soon after Mama went down & I had a great many treatments on them. If I don't work or walk and wear white cotton sox & tennis shoes I get along pretty well but the cold really gets to them – like today 15 below zero. God has been so good to us and that is the only way any of us really survived this summer. We think of you folks often and surely miss you all. Sylvia talks about it & the good times we had. She's been growing. Harry was fine a week ago. Love & prayers- us 3"

The facility was beautiful but my grandmother was not as wooed by its charms and conveniences as my mother thought, and so at least convinced herself that Grandma was happy. Grandma missed her independence sorely. She withdrew and died within a few years although she did truly need the care.

Myrtle, my Grandma Larsen's brother Floyd's widow, often came back to the area to visit her children, Eldon and Lila. Eldon, Myrtle's son, and his wife Vivian, owned a turkey farm. Since they needed to be near home to carry on the care of his flock, or "the correct name for a group of turkeys is a rafter you city slickers!" Eldon would correct us, the prime activity for these family reunions consisted of a picnic in the Perham Park. It was close enough to allow the McCulleys to tend to their responsibilities but far enough away from the farm aromas wafting from manure piles and the moldering turkey feed.

Art, Lila's husband, worked for the gas company and had some weekends off. They moved several places but always would come for these reunions. Art was Catholic so in general we avoided religion as a topic and scheduled activities to make sure they could get to

Mass. I always enjoyed the times with the first cousins once removed that I only saw once or twice a year. Sometimes my siblings would be present with the grandchildren and Mom was in her glory. Mom looked on Eldon and Lila more as siblings than cousins as my grandmother invited them to all occasions after their parents moved to Colorado for her brother's health needs just after the two oldest children left home.

Eldon taught us a lot about the turkey business and he would engage us in turkey-raising activities to help out so that he could enjoy free time during our visits. The turkeys he raised were broad-breasted white because they did not have unsightly pigment spots on their skin, making them more visually appealing, and they rendered an increased amount of meat.

We would walk through the barns filling the waterers and feeders and looking for any dead or sick birds. As we worked together Eldon would expound on all things turkey-related over the turkey gobbling cacophony. As a result, I seem to have more knowledge about turkeys than most. The juvenile females or jennies, are raised to about 15.5 pounds, which takes about 14 weeks and the young males or jakes, are raised to a market weight of 38 pounds, which takes around 18 weeks. The largest cost associated is feed and a young turkey eats twice its weight in feed before they are market- ready. My date and other visitors were sometimes enlisted to heft the heavy birds into the trucks when it was time to go to market. The production sheds were 60 feet wide and 528 feet long, not sure why the dimensions got stuck in my brain but they did! The sheds had huge fans and sides that could be raised for ventilation. My memory told me that each shed would have about 10,000 turkeys. I verified my facts with the National Turkey Federation and also learned that the newer operations are far more advanced from the days in the 1960's. The newer style turkey barns are windowless and fully automated with every element: food, water, light, waste management, and even loading on the trucks when they are finished to shorten the time to maturity resulting in greater profits.

Eldon was a fair-weather turkey grower and made no attempt to heat his production sheds for year-round meat production. He kept a few turkeys year-round for eggs in a more weather-tight heated shed and then would butcher them for personal use after they finished laying. It was interesting looking in the refrigerator at the huge dappled turkey eggs. Recipe adaptations were necessary if you were cooking with Vivian to accommodate the size of the eggs, usually about twice as large as a chicken egg. The standard picnic favorite of deviled eggs was not a dish that did well with the turkey eggs but egg salad was quick and easy. Turkey egg shells are thicker and are useful for a unique craft project. Vivian made jewelry boxes by carefully cutting the emptied egg shells in half either vertically or horizontally. A hole would be drilled in the top and bottom of the shell and the egg white and yoke blown out and collected for cooking or baking. She would use the egg in her cooking and then clean the eggshell halves well and dry completely. When the moment was right, she would line the eggshell with velvet, create a tiny hinge, pedestal and handle. The outside could be painted with a design or just shellacked to enhance the finish. I do not know what happened to the beautiful creations that my mom received from Vivian.

Violet Stende, was a cousin of my Grandma Larsen. Violet lived with her oldest son, Ray, on a farm near Flom Minnesota. Ray had two younger brothers who for all the years of my growing up lived in the Minneapolis area. Their father died when Ray was just 12 years old. Ray worked every day of his life from that time on till he was well over 90. Ray was a good cook. I remember delicious meals of smooth mashed potatoes, with absolutely no lumps, as he had riced them by hand before mashing them and adding lots of cream, butter, and salt. He would serve them up with fried chicken we watched him butcher with fresh or preserved vegetables or fruit he grew depending on the season. All this he did when he finished his farm work or paid job coming home to cook well after dark. He showed his love by feeding us. He cared dutifully for his mother and his younger brothers until they grew up and left the farm. Ray never married but continued to care for his mother and eked out a living by working the farm. When they struggled to make mortgage payments, he would take odd jobs. The situation worsened when Violet needed to be hospitalized and finally spent the last years of her life at Sunnyside Nursing Home. It was not discussed but likely she became a ward of the state. Ray lived in the neighborhood of my family up by Ulen and generally the distinctions between the Sanford relatives and the Larsen relatives weren't very clear cut.

Going to the Regiers was a frequent notation. Hazel, my dad's sister and her husband John and their children lived in a rented farm south of Ulen. Joanne and Harley, were five and eight years younger than I was respectively and we had many happy times together through the years despite whatever trials might be going on in the lives of our parents. The Regier family seldom went visiting anywhere themselves but we often went to their farm and enjoyed delicious meals of homemade bread, side pork and bounty from the garden. Whenever the relatives came from the west coast there would be a picnic at Uncle John and Aunt Hazel's house. We celebrated everything together. There was a note in Mom's diary that we celebrated Hazel's 53rd birthday at the farm on May 4, 1959.

Sometimes it was difficult to sort out who were relatives and who were friends mentioned in the diary entries.

My Aunt Alice often worked as a live-in caregiver for individuals and whoever she was caring for would get lumped in with the family gatherings. Since the people she cared for varied and had the same names as family members the distinctions were difficult.

Uncle Harry, my dad's only brother, stayed on the family farm east of Ulen, Minnesota, and was important in the childhood of all of the Eva Sanford offspring. There was always a dog, cat, an old horse, and colorful bantam (or banty chickens as we called them) to fascinate his beloved nieces and nephews. Dad would go out to the farm to help with fencing, haying, and grain harvest. Mom and I would try to clean up the kitchen enough to make a meal for the menfolk. As a bachelor farmer, he seemed to live on eggs and canned soup. The egg shells and soup cans would be stacked in the corner of the kitchen nearly to the ceiling. Mom also tried to take care of the laundry for him. No matter how much we cleaned and washed, it seemed the next time we were there, we saw no evidence of our efforts.

My usually upbeat mom made a notation that "these were hard days" one summer day when Frances Coalwell, the wife of dad's cousin, Dick, died tragically in an accident.

Visiting relatives was a summertime theme in the diaries. Several trips to Uncle Wallace, Grandpa Sanford's brother, and his wife Aunt Lucille, in Eugene, Oregon, were mentioned. Lucille was a smoker, not that common for a lady in those days, and she engaged in other scandalous habits such as drinking alcohol and having a cleaning lady.

It was a long drive, over 250 miles, to see Uncle John and Aunt Marian. Generally, we would drive after work one day arriving at my brother's home late in the evening. Hubert would cook us a huge breakfast and if he had the day off, he would join us for the hour's drive from Minneapolis to Northfield. Mom mentioned having a big ice cream cone for a meal on the road. My great Aunt Marian was the spitting image of my grandma Sanford, her sister. This physical resemblance as well as the fact that Aunt Marian had a special affection for my dad after the passing of her sister meant that we often made time to go visit despite whatever sacrifices were required. Dad and Aunt Marian also shared a love for baseball. There generally was a game on the radio in the background and all other activities ceased if there was an important moment in a game. Uncle John Thompson was a huge Swede who dwarfed his wife who was barely five feet in stature. This gentle giant, over six feet tall, thought the world of his wife although she was not your typical farm wife. She was an intellectual woman who loved to read. Her grey hair was drawn up in a loose bun and the soft hairs which came loose as she went about her day made a halo around her petite face. Marian's beautiful blue eyes were edged by well-earned laugh wrinkles and her diminutive chin was topped by a permanent Mona Lisa smile. Aunt Marian believes as Jean Houston, an author she enjoyed touted, "that at the height of laughter the universe is flung into a kaleidoscope of new possibilities". Uncle John and Aunt Marian ate most of their meals at the local diner or had simple fair at home on Sunday when the diner was closed. They were not churchgoers.

Mom admired my Aunt Marian and she was a role model for her in many ways. A significant way was the importance of higher education for her children. Three of Mom's children had started college and it seemed that there was not another proper choice in our household. Barbara and Shirley had their degrees and Hubert had an excellent career despite his lack of a degree. The Thompson children graduated from the consistently top-ranked Carleton College in nearby Northfield. The Thompsons shunned the more famous St. Olaf's College perhaps because it had been founded by Norwegian pastors. The diary entries regarding our visits commented that their son and daughter were not able to attend whatever event due to work. At the time I imagined they had important jobs in unidentified faraway places since no one took over the family farm which was the norm.

The farm was like no other I've ever been on. There were crews of hired hands that worked for Uncle John to grow, corn, peas, and carrots for Green Giant. During my childhood, I remember thinking he looked a lot like the green giant on the cans except for the fact he wasn't green. He was various shades of tan depending on how far up he rolled his sleeves. The top of his balding head and forehead were snowy white protected by his John Deere hat, which he rarely removed.

In nearby Manorville, about an hour drive further south, Grandma Sanford's brother, Claude and his wife, Rena, John Thompson's sister, resided. Uncle Claude was small of frame like his sisters and was long retired from working for the county road commissioner. He read and painted. Again, I wonder what happened to some of the paintings that he would do on scraps of Masonite. Aunt Rena was a sturdy woman somewhat taller than Uncle Claude. Aunt Rena cooked, canned and baked relentlessly. Meals in their home were a gastronomic delight.

In the same letter referenced earlier Mom talked about a blessed event where Aunt Rena's son Bill and his wife had a baby while in their forties. The letter read:

> "had a good note from Faye with their card & picture of Mark which we appreciated a great deal. It is so wonderful for them & Mark too."

June 26, 1966, marked Claude and Rena's 50th wedding anniversary. Dad came home at lunch the day before and we drove down and then stayed at the Sartell, Minnesota home of Art and Lila Kimmes. It was odd going the opposite direction starting in Mantorville and having to dress up and be part of the crowd.

Friends

"We are rather short on relatives in this area so were dependent on Friends to help out" Mom wrote in her letter to Aunt Rena. "One family of 5 moved into the upstairs part to help take care of Mama and help me. They pay for utilities and have it rent free- she is a very fine and conservative cook and good housekeeper-does our washing even shampoos my hair every week which is a great help to my arms. Mrs. June Collins has relatives in Minneapolis and Mankato where their son goes to his senior year in high school. Their oldest girl is in her second year of junior college in Fergus Falls. Mr. Lloyd Collins, is night clerk at the Graystone Hotel from 11 to 7 am. They have a girl in 6th grade at our ward school & 2 preschool boys 3 & 5. They have a farm home about 15 miles out so we were very fortunate to be have them to help us."

My folks met the Mastins when they moved to Detroit Lakes. Their kids were about the same age as my older siblings and helped them get settled in the nearby Washington elementary school when they made their mid-winter move. The two families worked on personal and church projects together so there weren't very many days that they didn't see each other. The Mastin's granddaughter, Beverly, was my age and they moved to Detroit Lakes in mid-September 1964 several weeks after school started when we were both in the 7th grade. Since we went to the same small church, we became fast friends. Bev remembers that I came to see her every day when she had an emergency appendectomy in the middle of a March 1966 blizzard when no one else could get out. A neighbor worked at the hospital and he would make tracks for me in the snow and I would spend the day with Bev and follow Duane home at the end of his shift. That cemented our relationship as 8th graders. There was a number of sleepovers trading off between our homes mentioned in diary notations. Bev's parents, Ivan and Gen, were my oldest sister's age. The couple bought my grandparent's farm sometime after my grandpa died. Dad was familiar with things and would offer advice and assistance with the much-needed renovations. We had three generations of fellowship with the Mastin family.

Neighbors

Neighbors were a big topic of the diary with activities as simple as sharing during one of the designated twice daily coffee times – forenoon or afternoon, and the occasional evening coffee. The coffee was generally made in an aluminum or enameled pot where water was boiled and a scoop of coffee, likely about 2 Tablespoons, was put into the boiling water, turned off and allowed to steep. As with all Minnesota activities, it required some finesse. The coffee could not boil for more than a few seconds or it would taste bitter, and the waiting time for it to settle to avoid disturbing the grounds when pouring had to be just right. Evening coffee Minnesota style was not likely to disturb anyone's sleep because it was so weak, but that was the specter that haunted everyone so evening coffee was generally reserved for an out-of-town guest who might have had a need to stay awake on the way home.

Bob Hill was another neighbor who did the carpenter work on the house at 222 East Main. Bob was a round kindly man with a white beard. The children in the neighborhood were in agreement that Bob was a code name and he was Santa Clause.

Most families lived down the street or a few miles away from any children who had left the nest. My mom and dad were always close to Bob because his son and my oldest sister Barbara lived in Oregon. Bob's son, Roy, was a fire smokejumper and lived in the northwest near Portland, where my sister lived. Bob would sometimes bring over clippings about happenings in that faraway land of Oregon. We would recount each piece of news to each other as part of our shared loneliness. We also shared good news, such as the birth of Bob's grandson and namesake, Robert Allen, on January 23, 1969. The grief of separation was largely unspoken but real. The grief seemed to relent a bit during the process of sharing with someone who understood the pain of being over 1,500 miles from some of the most important people in their lives, especially those little ones, so fresh from God.

The Poppenhagens were young by the neighborhood standards. Their son Philip was born on the 5th of January in 1967. My mother's position as Cradle Role chairwoman meshed with her role as neighbor and they became great friends. The next year in Mom's diary there was a notation of going to Philip Poppenhagen's first birthday party. In 1969 there was mention of the Poppenhagen's three kids so it was a prolific time for this young family. Rod Poppenhaggen was a roofer and a brief notation in the early 70's indicated he had fallen off a roof and died. Mrs. Poppenhaggen was still mentioned in diary entries right up until the end when Mom had her stroke and was unable to record in her diary.

Peggy Mackner owned the house next door. Peggy was a widow and rented out her upstairs for income but also for entertainment. She could be seen trekking up to the second floor to go through her renter's apartment if they vacated the premises for a few minutes. One clever renter actually set up a sting and pretended like he was going somewhere that would take a while and returned to catch her in the act of snooping. Most just put up with it as the rent was reasonable until they could find a place with more privacy. Peggy had a uniform spring, summer, and fall. She wore a sleeveless cotton print dress that she sewed herself. In the winter she added a sweater and anklet cotton socks to her outfit. Each morning she hung out her dress from the day before on the clothesline, along with her bra and bloomers. She would do her sheets once a week for a twin bed. It was all hand washed.

Peggy had a more efficient furnace than ours which burned natural gas. Her husband had built their new home just before he died. The basement had beautifully painted uniform concrete block walls and poured cement floor, not like our basement which was dug out of the earth with rickety wooden stairs and a few supports for the floor joists.

Peggy had a huge rag rug loom that she used to create rag rugs at any length you desired. She was losing her vision and my mom would assist her to thread the loom once every few months when she had exhausted the huge spools of thread. She spent many hours selecting and stitching together the rags that she wove into the rugs. The noise of the loom was considerable as she with her great strength and skill beat the fabric into the desired patterns with the warp and the woof.

The diary also contained names of those who had dropped by, letters or calls received on that day. Many of the names mentioned were unknown to me but for some reason had crossed paths with my mom who made note of their birth, death or coming by for coffee.

February marked the synchronized swimming contests. Our high school had a pool and hosted the competitions. Our neighbors, the Olsons, had daughters who participated in synchronized swimming. Mom would attend despite the fact that some of the church people disliked the idea on the grounds of lack of modesty. They didn't press the issue as even the most opposed to Mom's somewhat loose standards realized she was a valuable asset to the church and didn't openly criticize her for fear they would have to do the work themselves.

Neighbors also provided needed help in emergencies. There was a notation in February 1969, that Mrs. Olson "broke her leg in several places". Mom and Dad visited her in the hospital and did several things to provide for the needs of her children.

Acquaintances, Activity-Related Folks and Employers

Johnson Trucking was a family-owned business with Duane, the father, starting the excavating and hauling company with one truck many years before. Dewey, Duane's one and only son, became the boss. My dad faithfully worked hauling gravel, snow, rubble from buildings that were being torn down, mulch and stone for landscaping, or anything else that the company contracted to haul. In a letter Mom wrote to Aunt Rena in 1964 she mentioned some of her concerns about Dad's job: "Maybe Vance will be forced to retire from his job and we can have summer vacation time with the 3 of us with some time to stay & no hurried trips. Can't take so much excitement."

Dad would often take side work for other truck lines such as Daggett Trucking which hauled livestock. I remember overnight trips to the St. Paul stockyards asleep in the truck snuggled up to my dad.

Oscar Janke was a friend as well as an employer. He had been widowed for many years and owned several trucks. Dad was always glad to pick up some extra work from Oscar as his trucks were in good repair. He shared his love of cigars with my dad and was never seen without one. He also grew beautiful Canna lilies in his magnificent garden.

My mom made frequent mention in the summer of 1968 when I worked for the Moses family babysitting while Mrs. Moses went golfing during the day or out to adult activities in the evening. Mom chronicled each detail such as riding the 7.7 miles one way to work in the morning. Since my responsibilities also included cooking, typical to my mother's love of books, she bought me a joy of cooking book, which I use to this day. She mentioned my $15 per week salary proudly. The fact that I had no regular schedule chaffed her a bit. Their lake cabin was much nicer than anybody's home that we knew. Mr. Moses was an executive at a seed company in Fargo.

In a one-time-only entry, Mom mentioned they had gone to Stella Aune's auction and they heard about Emil Halderson. Who Stella and Emil were is a mystery and what in the world they heard about Emil was either confidential or space didn't allow for recording. There was a whole group of auction friends. Usually after an auction, my dad would be paid a small fee to clean up. You guessed it, many of those items would end up in our home, shed, yard, or be distributed among nearby relatives.

Mom's parent's wedding photo

Granny's Minnesota grandchildren

Mom's parents golden wedding anniversary

Birthday twin cousin Darlene Larsen | Ray Stende a McCulley cousin and Parnell Sanford

Eldon and Vivian | Jerry and Bev Olstead

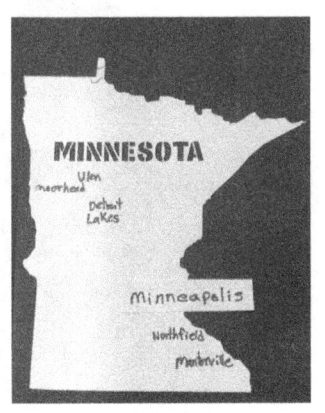

Aunt Marion and Daddy | Towns important to our family story

Uncle Claude and Aunt Rena's Golden Wedding Anniversary flanked by their siblings

Four generations at Emmauel

Lynne Huso and Eric Manchester, distance cousins who had never met but have a striking resemblance

Front Row L to right The Anfinson girls Kathy, Laura, Elaine "sissy" and Bev
Back row L to right The Anfinson boys John and David "Andy"

Deanna with dad Harvey Schlauderaff | Ivan and Gen Mastin

Daddy was always proud of the trucks he

Dad and Mom, 1972

Chapter 8
The Empty Nest and Beyond (1970-1979)

An empty nest is a household in which one or more parents live after the children have left home. At a young age, children are more dependent on their parents for every little thing, for their meals or studies. During the initial period for the Sanford family, I had varying degrees of awareness of the departure and transitions out of the nest for my older siblings as described in a previous chapter. I was growing up and living at home for the first eight years after the older siblings launched and I'm sure my presence blunted the pain of the older siblings leaving to a great extent. The main characteristic of empty nest syndrome described in the literature is that it is a sudden transformation. Empty nest syndrome has three stages: grief, relief, and joy. My parents' empty nest years continued and were not average. The fact that it was spread over many years makes it hard to identify stages. The only knowledge that I have is from the diaries.

Thanks to thepeoplehisotry.com we have some idea of what was going on in the world during the decade after the launching of the last child from the nest. A few highlights are:

> In 1971 The U.S. voting age was lowered from 21 to 18 years old when the 26th Amendment was ratified. This was just in time for the youngest member of the clan to exercise her right to vote for all the democrats per her Minnesota heritage.

In 1972 The Watergate Scandal began when White House operatives were caught burglarizing the Democratic National Committee. The Minnesota democrats were outraged. Mom and Dad went to Fargo to have the opportunity to meet "the next president of the United States of America", George McGovern. Sorry Mom!

In 1973 The United States Supreme Court declared that abortion was a constitutional right in the landmark decision on the Roe v. Wade. Most Minnesotans were outraged.

In 1974 U.S. President Richard Nixon resigned from office after being implicated in the Watergate Scandal. Minnesota Democrats rejoiced. Well, okay, Elmer Funkenheimier (actual name) was a little upset as he was one of the two Republicans in Becker County but no one liked him anyway!

In 1975 the movie "Jaws" opened in theaters. The landlocked Minnesotans renewed their vow to never mess around in the ocean. Minnesotans had always been wary of coastal living and preferred their position solidly in the middle with many beautiful lakes to enjoy with no large creatures lurking to devour them. The eighteen-page booklet prepared for the Ulen Diamond Jubilee in 1961 shed some light on the comfort of being in the middle. The book was mostly advertisements (thirteen of the inside pages plus three additional full-page advertisements, from prime sponsors, covering the inside of the bright orange card stock front cover and the front and back of the back cover). A unique feature on the lead page was a photo and biography of Ole Ulen, the town founder, written in Norwegian. Subsequent

The Empty Nest and Beyond (1970-1979)

pages included a poem, photos both past and present, as well as history and facts about Ulen. The leading fact about Ulen quoted with no corrections: "The village of Ulen is located in the northeastern part of Clay County, in western Minnesota, approximately 30 miles from the North Dakota border, and 150 miles south of the Canadian border. It lies nearly in the center of North America, lying midway between the Atlantic and the Pacific oceans, and equi distant from the Gulf of Mexico and the Hudson Bay." Minnesotans have had a long-standing love affair with the middle.

In 1976 Steve Jobs and Steve Wozniak created the Apple Computer Company. Most Minnesotans were oblivious.

In 1978 the computer video game Space Invaders was released. Minnesotans were ambivalent as they loved space but were confused about computers.

In 1979 The Three Mile Island nuclear incident occurred in Pennsylvania. Several nuclear power plants in Minnesota whose existence had been largely ignored previously suddenly became suspect.

Inflation was the biggest influence in the decade of the 1970's.

In 1970 a new house cost $23,400.00 and by 1979 was $58,500.00, more than double since the beginning of the decade. In 1970 the average income per year in the United States was $9,350.00 and by 1979 was $17,550.00.

In 1970 a gallon of gas was 36 cents and by 1979 was 86 cents.

> In 1970 the average cost of new car was $3,900.00 and by 1979 was $5,770.00.

Mysteriously, Mom paused in writing in her diary for exactly a year during the period when I left home in the fall of 1970. There was no diary record for 1970 except daily notes for the first month and a half (through February 14, 1970). These notes were scrawled on the memorandum pages at the end of the original volume which contained 1964-1969. When I began my studies at Olivet Nazarene College, pursuing a Bachelor of Science degree majoring in biology and minor in chemistry there were no diary notes. My mother started recording in her diary again on February 15, 1971.

This diary declared itself to be a five-year diary in no uncertain terms. Centered at the top of the title page the words shouting out in 20-point all-caps Times New Roman font:

FIVE YEAR DIARY

The two lines that followed were also centered but in much smaller font stating:

> "A Condensed Comparative Record for Five Years
> For Recording Events Most Worthy Remembering".

The most surprising feature below this inscription was a large circle graphically depicting the dozen astrological signs indicating the number of the house on the outermost ring of each wedge. The name of the period, a graphic depiction of the symbols, and the name of the graphic extended about halfway down the wedge. Each wedge segment had the start date for the sign represented on a line separating itself from the previous astrological sign. The central focus was a compass with the south indicator pointing slightly to the right of the middle top which we normally associate with the north. That seemed odd but I could hear my mother say "This thing is backwards!" I never knew

The Empty Nest and Beyond (1970-1979)

my mother to give any credence to horoscopes but her frugality likely overcame any reservations about the astrological stuff. Two full pages for each of the twelve astrological signs described the general characteristics of each together with implications for a person with that sign in each month of the calendar year filling pages 3-26. Mother was a Leo and I would agree that she was kind, sympathetic, and generous. Pages 27-32 contained items such as weather wisdom, an explanation of US standard time zones, weights and measures, legal holidays in various states, distances by boat between New York and other sea ports, birthstones by month and day of the week, monthly birthday flowers and wedding anniversaries. The final table was entitled "Foreign Cities, later than New York Time". Twenty-one cities were listed in alphabetical order from Antwerp to Vienna with two columns following. Neither column had a title heading. The first column I presume was the hours later but the second column of numbers was uninterpretable. It contained numbers from 1-57. Finally, I let loose of this futile waste of time to try to make sense of this table and moved on. The previous owner of the diary Mom began to use in 1971 evidently tore out the pages previous to February 8th. I imagined that these pages may have included some personal notes. It could have been my mom who removed the early pages as she was no stranger to using scotch tape to secure gaps where pages had been removed or had come loose. Inexplicably, Mom left seven full pages entirely blank at the beginning and began recording on February 15, 1971.

The diary did show more personalized glimpses into these years beyond the empty nest. I found myself frustrated as I had very limited recollections of a few shared experiences during these years. Even though the first in the series of the three books that contained the record of the years 1971 to 1979 had boldly announced itself as a five-year diary, curiously, my mother ignored the four-line designations for each year and instead used the full page for chronicling the happenings of 1971. Many of the diary entries contained the same mundane information but they had a different tone. Mom seemed lonely. For the first time a list of TV programs watched appeared almost every day. The daily notations included jottings about letters to and from the children and other friends and relatives. Even this aspect was a bit different as she would include notes that expressed disappointment about not receiving a letter from a certain person, "I haven't heard from _____ in a long time".

Mom and Dad were always willing to welcome me home whenever I could make the trip from college. On February 20, 1971, my mom wrote "Syl's friends Doris and Deloris Schlagle made the trip home with her. They had fun snowmobiling at Allan's". We were really ahead of the curve as snowmobiles were generally just farm machinery at that time and had not been embraced as a recreational vehicle.

Mom's physical condition seemed to be declining. One stretch of not feeling well lasted several weeks beginning on February 25, 1971, her sister Evelyn's 56th birthday. She wrote, "discovered that I was too shaky to go out for coffee". Sunday, February 28, 1971, she wrote "Called Mastins as I was too tired to go out". I assume the Mastins were going to pick Mom up for church as there was no car running at that time. March 3, 1971, she wrote, "just flaked out & went to bed and ate country cornflakes late". March 7, 1971, Mom wrote "I felt so rank & wondered if I could make it to church, I did and enjoyed the services though I was way too tired & too nervous for anyone's good". Wednesday, March 10th, 1971, Mom wrote "felt rotten so stayed home from NWMS meeting. Vance took reports for church to Mastins. Greased up and went to bed". Mom's words on March 14th, 1971, indicated a worsening of her symptoms "Woke up sick and couldn't be up". Finally, March 15, 1971, Mom sought medical help "10 am appointment at clinic & I am glad to go. Glad to have pap test out of the way & medicine included".

In previous years' diaries there had never been a mention of her poverty. On March 9, 1971, Mom wrote, "Eva came & we took off for antique shop after coffee. Also, to Penny's, R&S fabric and me with no money." April 28th, 1971, "Bill from clinic of $109 plus not counting last time". On the same day she included the fact that the kitchen roof had a leak and repairs were needed commenting "I am so shook up about the kitchen".

The Empty Nest and Beyond (1970-1979)

The whole of my spring vacation it snowed and I had to walk to work several days as we could not get the car out. I went back to college on April 12th and on the 17th, there was a tornado warning. Aww the joys of Minnesota weather!

I came home from college for the summer on May 13, 1971, flying into Fargo late in the evening. Mom and Dad planned to leave for Portland on June 9th. The weeks in between my arrival and their departure were busy with visiting, the usual spring routine to open the upstairs rooms, getting the yard ready and me working as many hours as I could. Mom's diary pages were filled with the fun of joining in the end of school activities with neighborhood and church kids. The early days of June were spent washing clothes and packing for the trip. Quitting work at lunchtime on the 8th Dad came home and got cleaned up and they hit the road for Minneapolis. Hubert continued to work for Northwest Airlines, but did not purchase another home to renovate. He was very attentive to Mom and Dad facilitating travel early in the decade.

The flight on the 9th was "smooth" with no delays and they arrived in time for dinner in Portland with the Manchester family. Art was teaching German and Barbara was at the end of her career working as a teacher's aide with the developmentally disabled class at the Gresham high school.

The next morning was breakfast with the kids and teachers on the last day of Vance's first-grade year with little brother Eric in tow. Church activities, family fun, and Amway business filled a week before Mom and Dad left for Eugene. There were visits to see Dad's sisters, nieces, nephews, cousins, and other assorted friends and shirt-tail relatives. He had been feeling "poorly" and had not gotten his Valium prescription filled so it was noted in several stops that three family members provided Valium from their supply. My parents returned on June 22nd to Portland and enjoyed family times and getting ready for the next adventure, a trek to Canada to see their daughter Shirley. One of the pre-trip activities was sorting through Barb's stash of baby clothes to take along as Shirley was expecting. Although Howard pipelined his entire life, he had several forays into other businesses. In the early '70s he started Columbia Airlines in Northern British Columbia, Canada.

June 27th was a busy day with packing up and heading to church, over a 30-minute one-way trip. Manchester time was slow and often tardiness was the rule rather than the exception. There might have been some miscommunication as Edie did not bring the distinctive baby gift to church. Barb's traditional baby gift for special friends and relatives was a hand-knitted sweater set created by her English war bride church friend, Edie. The ever-gracious Edie invited the Manchester sextet to her home for lunch and they could pick up the gift. Fortunately, Edie's husband, Harold, was a mechanic who was able to solve a car problem that needed attention before they left on the trip. A common entry in her diary was the statement "this was God's provision!" on this day and many others as she truly believed it with all of her heart.

The entourage left for Canada at four in the afternoon and arrived at Marg and Laurie Alho's home around 11 p.m. Marg was Howard's sister. They much enjoyed a late dinner of KFC before collapsing into the beds prepared for them. Mom commented on how much she enjoyed the boys, Rolland, Neil and Dale. The next morning everyone enjoyed a beautiful breakfast buffet of waffles, fruit, bacon and juices. Marge packed a lunch with the leftovers from the night before, and included a jug of fresh squeezed lemonade, when she sent the refreshed travelers on their way at 10 a.m. Mom had suffered from the mountain roads the day before and dreaded getting back on the road again but remarked in her diary "the road changed shortly and the flat farm lands were a joy". The group arrived in Prince George at about 10 p.m. to a candlelight dinner of spaghetti and all the trimmings beautifully served in true Metcalfe style. The cousins had great fun playing together and the accommodations were pronounced "good".

The morning after their arrival there was a repeat of the waffle buffet and afterwards all four of the Manchester family, Dad and Howard with his kids in tow went out to the airport. Mom and Shirley stayed behind to unpack. Lunch was mentioned but not completely described. Dinner was "pork chops and the works". Other dinner guests were

The Empty Nest and Beyond (1970-1979)

former distributors so Art and Barb "thoroughly discussed Amway" long after Howard had gone to bed with Mom wistfully longing to go to bed herself.

The June 30th breakfast was described as good with no details. Lunch was tea at a special market and dinner was roast beef at the Metcalfe residence. The evening conversation with different guests was described as "better" perhaps because it did not delay bedtime and the stereo wasn't "blaring". July 1st was a holiday, Dominion Day. The sleet did not favor the planned cookout so all ten went into town for lunch and minor sightseeing. The best part in Mom's view was returning home, eating a quick bite, and going to bed early. The next morning dad did some handyman jobs and it was a low-key day. Saturday the third the picnic was rescheduled and enjoyed with some unnamed out-of-town guests. Sunday morning, Barb and Shirley sang a duet at church and all enjoyed a family dinner with gift giving with exotic items from Iran and unidentified "goodies" that Mom had brought from home. The items had weathered the trip well and all seemed "happy" with what they received. After lunch the travelers headed south again. The rainy weather made driving difficult and they arrived at an "expensive" hotel at midnight. The next day there was a visit with cousins Della and Francis in Tacoma on the way to Portland. Art's sister Pat came over for an evening visit and it was "1:30 am before we hit the hay". The next day Mom did laundry and got all packed up. The plane left on the 7th and Hub picked them up in Minneapolis. July 8^{th,} they arrived home to a house Hub and I had been working on since they left. Mom's diary read "Words fail me when I try to tell all that has been done at home in the house, but sufficient to say it is like a new place". The next day a list of many people dropped by to come see the renovations. Hub and I had kept them at bay so Mom and Dad would be the first to see. Mom also noted she wrote letters to share the news about the house remodel. Most of the following days included notes about unpacking and reorganizing items in the newly renovated home and receiving guests for a tour. July 27th, Mom's two sisters and several nieces arrived with a "nice spread of hotdish, raspberries, cake and cream" to celebrate mom's 60th birthday.

The remodeling drama that occurred in their absence was much better unobserved. I worked 3-11 shift most days. I would sometimes be called in 4 hours early or stay as many as eight hours late. One night when I came in from work at 11:30 having worked 12 hours that day Hub looked at me and said "I wonder what this room would look like without that wall." He got up with his crowbar and I followed with mine and in less than an hour we had the wall with the large archway between the living room and dining room out of the way. This was the heyday of wood paneling which meant we just paneled over everything and no one was the wiser of what lurked behind the fresh looking exterior. I learned about all kinds of products such as a liquid wood concoction that we mixed up and just poured into several of the low corners in the end of the room to level it. The cover up solution for the floors was carpet over everything. We fortunately had a discreet cousin who was a carpet layer so he gave us a good price and did the work. The ceiling was a different matter. We worked many long hours on getting the suspended ceiling to at least look straight. In the 30 days they were gone everything had been done. Hubert was the general contractor and I was the apprentice. He had honed his skills over the last 20 years of house flipping. It was great fun! Hubert would make huge batches of something we could eat; his specialty was tuna salad with ring macaroni. We would just eat whatever he made until it was gone. We even went to church a few times together and nursed a stray kitten back to health. Truly sibling bonding time.

After the return home from the big trip the diary went back to the mundane items with many days of looking for car parts and taking the battery from one car to another in an effort to get one of the fleet of cars to work. One note showed a little irritation from Mom that Dad had tied a rope around the muffler because the car frame was too rusted out to hold the screws. "He expected me to hold onto the rope to keep the muffler from dragging on the ground all the way to Ulen!" The goal for

The Empty Nest and Beyond (1970-1979)

the day was to try to piece together more suitable transportation from the additional cars available on the farm.

The number of days that mom reported feeling sick or staying in bed all day and not dressing appeared to increase. September 16, 1971, she wrote "In the morning there is always the diary & bible reading dishes & handwash. Thought of desperation in prayer". Tuesday, October 16, 1971, mom wrote "sat up dizzy, stood up dizzy, then laid down & house moved around. One never knows". October 28th, 1971, painted a bleak picture "We never decide to go to the Dr. or get anyone to help with Northside house papering & fixing basement pipes so they won't freeze. That mess upstairs gets to me more & more-especially as cold descends on us. God help me & us both."

December 12, 1971, Mom's diary note read "Shirley & Howard called about 1030 pm about Michael Lester born at 5pm & weighed 7# 3 oz". December 19th, Mom noted "Jennie, Diane & Sylvia came around 9p & did stop for lefse & pumpkin pie & coffee. Sylvia goes to work at 645am". I worked most days but took time for sledding or skating with friends. I had Christmas day off and we went to the Regiers. The 1971 diary ended with notes in the last pages that ran through January 14, 1972. Interestingly, she also had a separate volume that began on January 1st, 1972. I compared the duplicate entries and they were nearly identical.

April 1972 was Mom noted "I enjoyed a tour of the Betty Crocker test kitchens in Minneapolis with Sylvia's college friends, Dorcas Ross, a home economics major and her roommate, Ann Seaney. They had come home to Minnesota with Syl for Easter vacation". In addition to the tour and church activities we made a run to Winnipeg, Manitoba, a first time visit to Canada for both ladies and built a snow Easter bunny, also a first for them.

"Sylvia called to say she was engaged" appeared in my mom's diary on April 15, 1972. Other following notes through the spring and summer gave details such as "put in engagement announcement" on May 30th.

Mom noted in her diary on April 30th "Syl changed her major to nursing". The backstory was that in the spring semester of 1972, I was struggling with two required courses, physical chemistry, and molecular biology. It appears that P Chem and Molecular Bio are only thinly disguised math, not my forte. Discouragement quickly escalated to despair when I was declined admission to the Physical Therapy School at Loma Linda University where I had planned to begin in the fall. One beautiful Saturday morning when other students were out lollygagging around, I was inside setting up for a vertebrate zoology lab and opened a 55-gallon drum of sharks that had not been properly preserved. The smell was foul and by the time I finished disposing of the varmints and found a substitute for the lab I was almost late for dinner to Mrs. Howe, a family friend from Minnesota. Lettie, as she urged me to call her, and I never quite could, served as faculty in the home economics department at Olivet. Previously, she was at NNC where my sisters both enjoyed her delicious dinners with a collection of other guests. Mrs. Howe listened carefully about my terrible, horrible, no good, very bad day as I was the only guest that evening. She gave me her full attention and queried about my studies. At a subsequent dinner, she invited a nursing professor, Dr. Catron. During the course of that evening, I began to realize that nurses could be very different from the nurses I worked the evening and night shifts with when I was a nurse's aide at the rehab hospital in Northern Minnesota. Dr. Catron talked about the new opportunity to take the freshman and sophomore nursing curriculum integrated into one course in the summer of 1972. Mrs. Howe admitted later that it was a set up but she offered to allow me to stay in her home rent-free that summer when I took the course. How could I say no?

    My fiancé drove me home to meet my family after my summer nursing course. We had a family portrait taken at that time. My usually agreeable mother was very insistent that the photo included "just my kids and grandkids" not my fiancé was unspoken, but understood.

    The time was fun with all the Manchester and Metcalfe cousins enjoying a time of togetherness at Hub's house in Minneapolis as well as times at the farms "up north" owned by family. A go-cart was built by Grandpa Vance for the occasion and the four oldest cousins remember to this day, over 50 years later, all the fun they had.

The Empty Nest and Beyond (1970-1979)

My fiancé, was not able to come back to school in the fall. He was putting some pressure on me to get married sooner, not after my graduation as originally planned. He intended for us to move near his home and family and continue school there. Mom must have been in constant prayer but never pointed out her concerns. It was decided that I would spend Christmas at my fiancé's parents' home.

At some point in the early hours of the New Year a discussion occurred that clearly demonstrated we did not have similar lifetime goals and he left in a huff to return to his apartment. His sister took me to the airport to fly to Minneapolis early on New Year's Day. I left the engagement ring on the dresser of his parent's guest room and never looked back. One of the points of contention was he did not "approve" of my going on a student mission core assignment for the summer of 1973. God had a different plan and I went on that trip and it changed my life in many ways. Thank you, Mom, for your prayers and support.

The five-year diary that picked up on January 1st of 1973 had some water damage which made many of the entries along the edges illegible. In my usual quest for perfection, I was discouraged but forged ahead.

In 1973 there were two new party marketing opportunities mentioned for the first time, "decorating party" later identified as Home Interiors and "jewelry party" later specified as Sarah Coventry. The old standards of visits from the Avon lady, Stanley home products and Tupperware remained and were mentioned frequently.

There was at least one pipe freezing episode recorded in January or February in every year through the decade of the 70's. This explained my mom's concern over not getting someone to do the necessary winterizing when Dad was too sick to accomplish the important tasks. The cold seemed to exacerbate all the household issues and complicate every event. The midnight arrival of the Metcalfe family on January 6, 1974, in bad weather when the pipes had frozen was one example. Mom pronounced the event as "chaos" but the next day she wrote "The living word is a thrill to read." She truly was a woman of faith!

In 1974 mention of going to "the center" became a frequent diary entry. The old high school that my mom and all of us attended at various points in our educational endeavors had been transformed into a senior center. At the center lunch was served, various activities were enjoyed, and trips for seniors were planned and facilitated. Mom played in the center kitchen band called the Ding-a-Lings. In good weather, they would play at festivals, fairs, or other events. They would attend the funerals of members and friends of the band decked out in their red and white uniforms. Mother didn't miss many funerals it seemed. She also attended those of individuals affiliated with the Women's' Christian Temperance Union (W.C.T.U.) in some manner. The members each wore the organization's distinctive white ribbon. There was an accompanying brochure that was laid at the desk with the funeral folders to make people aware of the work of the W.C.T.U.

As the years progressed more and more often her notes read "Vance down carried lunches". Hub's role began to transition to assisting with things at home as Dad's COPD worsened and limited their travel.

March 27, 1974, Mom wrote "Weather is surely a problem but God controls weather too." At the end of the ten weeks of the intensive course I returned home for a brief visit in late August. A chance meeting with my high school debate colleague, Paul Benshoff, resulted in a wonderful job opportunity. Paul's mother, Helen Benshoff, was director of nursing at Multi-County Nursing Service, which served three northern Minnesota counties (Becker, Mahnomen, & Hubbard) and had its main office in Detroit Lakes. Helen had written a grant that would provide some financial support for a nurse intern for two years during study at a university in return for coming to work upon graduation at the agency. The opportunity also provided for training and work during vacations before graduation. This seemed to me like an answer to prayer. I was in! The last two years of study flew by and the next thing I knew was approaching graduation. My dream job, with the wonderful colleagues that I had come to love over the last two years, would begin right after graduation and I felt it was too good to be true. January 2nd 1974 when I came to work at the agency Helen did not seem like her usual perky self. She asked me to come into her office. Helen began, "It is very hard to have to tell you this but our funding has been reduced and after you

The Empty Nest and Beyond (1970-1979)

finish as vacation relief staff in August, I cannot afford to keep you on. I am so sorry." Her words were barely audible. She was holding back the tears that glistened in her eyes. I was stunned but said, "I understand" when I really didn't. As I got my assignment and headed toward the first patient's home in the blustery winter weather the reality was beginning to hit me. It was expensive to live in the area. I looked for other jobs but could not find anything that would be able to support me and pay my school loans which would be coming due in a few months following graduation. The pain of this crushing blow intensified as my efforts to find a job in the area would require a one hour commute each way and would still not allow me to afford to buy a car. I was borrowing my brother's car until I could afford one. The original plan was to live at home until I could buy a car. Apartments were expensive in the area not to mention utilities. The next week I trudged through like a good soldier at work and returned to college with a heavy heart.

Just about the time I was sinking into despair, as fate would have it, Cheryl Roat came to speak to our senior seminar class at Olivet about a teaching job at Graham Hospital School of Nursing in Canton, Illinois. Having a Bachelor's degree in nursing was a prize at that time. I went for an interview and learned there were two jobs. I reached out to my former Resident Assistant, Debbie Potbury, and learned she was looking for a job outside of Ohio as she had broken up with her boyfriend. Canton was about halfway between Detroit Lakes and St. Mary's, Ohio, where Debbie was living. Debbie agreed to consider this opportunity. About a week after my interview, I received a letter from the Nazarene pastor in Canton, Rev. Norman Chandler. It seemed that Betty Stockov, the director of the school of nursing, did her homework and contacted the pastor after the interview. It seemed like a sign that we should move there.

My graduation from college was May 24th, 1974. Hugh brought Mom and Dad. Mom's only notation about all the activities was "Sat with the Seaney's". The mistress of understatement!

By the time August rolled around Debbie had gotten back with her boyfriend. When I went in to ask Helen to be released from my job the beginning of August instead of the end of the month, she told me that she had managed to find funding for continuing my position but it was too late. My employment contract and a lease for an apartment had been signed so there was no going back, only forward. We struggled to move ahead to what had seemed like divine intervention only a few months ago.

After my last day of work my brother Hubert loaded up a U-Haul trailer and we hit the road. We arrived at his house late Friday evening. At the crack of dawn, we left his home and hoped to make the nearly 500-mile trek that day. We traveled during a gas shortage. Despite being unable to get gas at several places we miraculously made it to Galesburg, Illinois, 41 miles from Canton. We needed more gas but the gas stations closed at 6 p.m. so we were forced to get a motel. The next morning, we obtained fuel, drove to Canton, and found the apartment. The two of us unloaded all my earthly belongings from the trailer up the four flights of outside stairs. Debbie and I took up residence in our apartment at 232 West Chestnut with furnishings we had brought from home.

Life in Canton was good and I met, Rod Heinze, the love of my life, at church. He seemed more convinced than I was about our relationship initially and when trying to rebuff his offer of a ride in the Cadillac he pretended was his I made the now famous remark, "Firefighters don't drive Cadillacs". We had our first date in October and our second in February. I told my mom in a letter home "this relationship isn't going anywhere no matter how hard he tries". When Mom questioned me in a later letter "Are things getting serious?" I replied "he grows on you".

January, 15, 1975, Mom wrote "dad got Sylvia a ride back to Illinois with a truck driver but the truck could not get under a viaduct so she took the bus from Chicago she called home safe."

The summer diary entries in 1975 were focused on Rod who had proposed to me on June 1st and I said yes and called my parents on June 2nd. The end of June he made the trek to meet my parents. We drove from my former roommate Debbie's wedding in Ohio, and arrived on June 29th. We made the traditional trip to the headwaters of the Mississippi at Lake Itasca and visited with friends and relatives in the

The Empty Nest and Beyond (1970-1979)

area. July 2nd Rod flew out of Fargo despite flooding and a tornado. July 4th, Mom, Dad and I loaded into my 1970 Ford Torino to head west. The car had a black vinyl roof and no air conditioning. In later years when it was used by one of Rod's summer college salesmen it was dubbed "the Sahara". Many of the people and places mentioned in previous trips were revisited but we made two first time visits: one to Lake Louise and the other to Lake Moraine, "truly stunning!" We returned to Detroit Lakes on July 27th. Mom noted in her diary on July 28th, 1975 "Rod called to tell Sylvia he had bought a house." The next day her entry read "Sylvia left for Illinois today she starts back to work on Monday. Hard to say goodbye to see her make such a long trip on her own and we will be so lonesome".

A particularly frightening diary entry for me was on September 15th, 1975, "I couldn't get up to the bathroom, Jeannette brought a commode."

Rodney Wesley Heinze and I planned to be married on December 20, 1975. The Canton First Church of the Nazarene blew away in a tornado in July so the venue was changed to the Assemblies of God Church. Several conservative Nazarene of our acquaintance cautioned, "you don't want to get mixed up with that bunch as they're tongues!" Several others felt like we should wait till our new church was finished and "it shouldn't take very long".

Throwing caution to the wind we were married at the Assembly of God Church in Canton. The song that my mother introduced me to many years earlier, "They'll Know We are Christians by our Love", not exactly a traditional wedding song, was sung by Rod's cousin Flora, in her beautiful soprano voice.

Hub dutifully brought the parents as well as my friend Bonnie Hoglum to the ceremony. Sister Barbara was able to make the trip. The house that Rod bought narrowly missed having the same fate as the church and became a haven for the out-of-town family who came for the nuptials.

The number of notations "Vance down" from my estimation was about 50 percent of the days in 1976. There seemed to be a steady increase of about 10 percent per year until 80 percent of the time

Daddy was "down". February 29, 1976, Mom wrote "been cutting down on cookies and salt in cooking", seemingly making an effort at some healthier eating. March 1, 1976, the depth of Mom's concerns about her health were illustrated "Today still down and Vance really going around. Really nerve wrecking all ideas about fixing upstairs and down scares me to an absolute frazzle when I am not feeling well".

In 1976 Wesley and Company, Rod's business purchased a 15-passenger Ford van. Dad loved the new vehicle and took great pride in riding shotgun around the countryside during the visit home that summer. When we left Dad insisted that we load up a dining table, six chairs and a hutch that he knew I'd always liked. He was an expert packer and so proud of everything that he was able to pack into the van.

Shortly after this trip, we learned I was pregnant. Our schedules were full and we deferred tentative travel plans to Minnesota for Christmas. The alternate plan was to have my parents have a nice trip and then come help with the new baby. Mom and Dad started their trip in February and made the rounds first to Osoyoos, British Columbia, Canada, on the south end of the Okanagan Valley. Howard had accepted a teaching position there and he and Shirley were beginning to consider where they might want to purchase a home.

Adam Wesley Heinze was born March 9, 1977, three weeks early. "Baby Adam" (as a few still call him today) did not wait till his due date, March 20th, his grandpa Adam's birthday. My parents did not know about the birth until about a week later as they were on the Hawaii leg of "the nice trip" and were staying at a hotel named the "Coral something" according to my sister Barbara. Sadly, Barbara had misplaced the actual note with the name of the hotel and phone number. Calling the over 200 hotels with "coral" in the name in Honolulu did not seem like a practical option. Mom noted in her diary on March 16, 1977, "Got news of Adam Wesley Heinze born March 9".

Rod came to the delivery at the end of his 24-hour shift at the fire department and went home exhausted after the birth. Friends went to check on him when he did not answer the phone and found him delirious with a fever and called the ambulance. He was hospitalized with

The Empty Nest and Beyond (1970-1979)

pneumonia and could not come to visit and anyone that saw him on the 1st floor could not get up to see me in the OB unit located on the 3rd floor. When I was discharged Rod's parents came to care for me. I was sad and lonely.

Hubert acting as the transportation coordinator as usual made sure that the folks did make it to Adam's dedication at our church in Canton on April 3rd. The trials of the last weeks surrounding Adam's birth seemed to disappear in the joy of being together.

I did not go back to teaching at Graham after Adam was born but had a happy life of going to parks and taking walks with a son who slept through the night from the time he was six weeks old. We packed him along everywhere we went. He was the prince of the church and charmed all with his smile. We made a trip home to Minnesota in the summer of 1977 when Adam was 6 months old. All the Minnesota friends and relatives enjoyed meeting the youngest member of the family and didn't even notice the many mosquito bites he collected, but his father was shocked and not so understanding of the Minnesota state bird preying on his precious son.

The opportunities for the Sanford family to see their grandchildren were limited due to distance. Enjoyment of times together were exponentially increased by the infrequency. The photo below evidenced Vance's affection for his two youngest grandsons. The photo was taken at Daddy's 75th birthday celebration, which Hubert hosted at his home in Minneapolis.

Mom noted on January 1, 1978, that she started to read the Bible through this year. There were not many remarkable events recorded in 1978 but the same list of who visited, called, chores and lists of activities. On December 31st she proudly noted that she had "completed bible reading with Revelation 20, 21, and 22".

For the first 27 months of Adam's life Rod's parents saw him almost every week. Grandpa Adam would bring his tools and his jars and cans of screws and nails and would do many handyman jobs. Baby Adam was his biggest fan until June 6th, 1979, when mom noted "Adam Heinze died".

Daddy's 75th birthday party, April 19th, 1979

Two youngest grandchildren Michael Metcalfe (L) and Adam Heinze (R)

Eva and Elmer Schimming, April 16th, 1980.

CHAPTER 9
LIFE AFTER VANCE (1979-1993)

The beginning of the end for Daddy was June 10, 1979, Mom noted "Vance really having breathing trouble." June 22, 1979, Daddy went up to the clinic in Fargo and was subsequently admitted to St. Luke's Hospital for testing. It seems that he might have taken the medical transportation bus and Mom stayed home to do some banking and pick up prescriptions on foot. On the morning of June 25th when Mom called to talk to Daddy on the phone, it turned out to be the last time she would hear her husband's voice. Mom also was able to speak with Dr. Spellman, the cardiologist. Dr. Spellman told Mom that Daddy had congestive heart failure brought on and masked by his emphysema. Mom went with her sister-in-law Alice to take Hazel, Daddy's sister, and Joanne Regier her daughter, to Fergus Falls for a hearing for Hazel's husband John. Later that day when Mom called Daddy's room to tell him the outcome of the hearing his roommate answered and said they had moved him "in a hurry". Alice dropped Hazel and Joanne home in Hawley and she and Mom went to St. Luke's and stayed. Sadly, Daddy was unresponsive when they arrived. For the next 36 hours, they alternated visiting him for ten minutes every two hours at the top of the even hours. The intensive care unit was a difficult place. After her 8 a.m. visit on June 27, 1979, Alice took Mom home to an empty house. Mom made phone calls. During those conversations, she told her children for the first time about the seriousness of the situation. Brother Hubert made the flight arrangements and I arrived at 3 in the morning on Thursday morning June 28th with two-year-old Adam in tow. Sister

Barbara arrived at 3 that afternoon and Shirley arrived a day or two later. The diary entries for the next month centered on where we slept, who came by, and what, and with whom we ate. July 5th Mom noted, "today is tracheostomy day". Since I was the youngest, I would usually get Adam to sleep in the room we had rented for the night and walk back to the hospital to sleep on the couch in the family room. After ten days and no changes I returned home to Illinois with Adam so that Mom could get a smaller room. Also, it relieved the stress of having someone responsible for a two-year-old in the mix of everything else that was happening. July 18th, Barb stayed all night as Dad had seizures. Barb and Shirley both left by the 25th of July. Hubert came and took Mom home to check on things. On July 28th Mom's diary read "St. Lukes called at 230am, Hugh and I to St. Lukes until about 2 o'clock. Daddy died. Lunch and birthday cake at Joanne's then home. I am 68."

Diary entry for August 1, 1979, read simply "Vance's final day on earth".

August 2, 1979, the entry was "Howard got word on Saudi Arabia so 6 went back to Canada". We had several days of trips with the Manchester family and on the 6th of August Mom recorded "Sylvia, Rod and Adam left for home".

Mom as a widow was a very different person. She took to her new responsibilities well. The notation for August 9th was "death certificate. Can't get Shirley for her 43rd". August 13th the diary recorded "paid for grave stones for Vance and John Peter". Daddy had gotten a good-sized scrap piece of blue tile from the façade of the hospital and this had marked John Peter's grave for over 25 years. It was a source of contention for the pair but Mom took care of that in one fell swoop. She was tying up loose ends as the August 16 diary record read "got a will for me $50".

Mom would send interesting little sayings in her letters to me as clippings or in her sometimes cryptically illegible cipher or mentioned them in phone conversations. These are a few of my favorites that came to my mind, recounted to my best recollection:

- I'm at that age where my mind still thinks I'm 29, my humor suggests I'm 12, while my body mostly keeps asking if I'm sure I'm not dead yet.
- We all get heavier as we get older, because there's a lot more information in our heads. That's my story and I'm sticking to it.
- When I was a kid, I wanted to be older... this is not what I expected.
- Life is like a helicopter. I don't know how to operate a helicopter.
- It's probably my age that tricks people into thinking I'm an adult.
- Just remember, once you're over the hill, you begin to pick up speed.
- I'm getting tired of being part of a major historical event.

The responsibilities of caring for Vance in his declining health had severely curtailed my parents' travels and other activities. As soon as the details concerning Daddy's death were taken care of Mom took a trip to Portland, Oregon. On that trip, Barb and Art tried to "fix her up" with their beloved widowed friend Charlie Blaylock. Charlie's wife, Jenny, had been the babysitter for the Manchester boys through the years and they served as surrogate grandparents. The Blaylock family attended Brentwood Church of the Nazarene and were family in many ways. Charlie was greatly saddened by the passing of his wife. Mom wasn't ready to be fixed up but it might have started her on the road to dating. September 26, 1979, she started to change all that and recorded "date for dinner and dance". A few days later on October 1 she stated for the first time in a series of days "shot my mouth off again" which might have referred to her now famous retort "Vance is just as dead as he is ever going to be" if someone inquired about her dating so soon.

Even though she was now single and her social life blossoming it was not a panacea. January 11, 1980, she wrote "broken water pipe upstairs shut off water". January 12, she wrote "no Leo", her beau, even though she had called him on the eleventh. Bad Leo. The first mention of the man she would later marry was on January 12, 1980 "Elmer

S called'. On the 4th of February Mom went to church with Elmer at the Seventh Day Adventist Church (S.D.A).

On February 22, 1980, the US Olympic Hockey team triumphed over the Russian team. This victory was called the miracle on ice. Minnesotans are great hockey fans so it was interpreted as a good omen for the year.

February 23rd Mom wrote "Blacked out at SDA prayer meeting ended up in ER. Elmer stayed." The mention of Elmer became more and more frequent with big events like celebrating his 60th birthday on February 29th or a little kindness he extended when The April 3rd entry read "Elmer weeding the yard." The turning point in their relationship occurred on April 5th when Mom wrote "went to foot washing and communion. Realized I need Elmer." Mom recorded on the 10th "Elmer and I to Hawley. Applied for marriage license $15 rings cheap $125". April 15th "Big announcement at center" and April 16th "Big day of getting married." On the 17th she made a note "called Hugh and hotline." Rod had an 800 number for his business which Mom called the hotline. The new secretary answered and Mom blurted out "This is Sylvia's mother. Please tell Sylvia I got married to Elmer yesterday" and hung up. Judy became a friend. Now in retrospect, a good friend who had many good laughs with me, after her initial shock wore off and the awkwardness of delivering the message was behind us.

Three days after the nuptials On April 19, 1980, Mom wrote "Sylvia called Rachel Jessie born 630 am today". This day was Daddy's birthday, the first since his death. On May 1, 1980, "wedding reception at the SDA". Church attendance at least doubled for the couple as they attended the S.D.A. on Saturday, the Sabbath, two services, morning and evening, with a repeat at the Nazarene Church on Sunday. There were also midweek services at both churches as well as lending a hand with projects taken on by the congregants at the S.D.A. and the Detroit Lakes Church of the Nazarene. Various area nursing homes had services from both churches and Mom mentioned singing at those services with the group that went from the Nazarene and S.D.A. to lead the services. On May 9, 1980, Mom and Elmer headed to Illinois with Hugh. The trip included the dedication of Rachel, on Mother's Day. Rachel was dressed in the same dress for her dedication that I was for mine.

May 18, 1980, Mount Saint Helen erupted for the first time in 100 years, raining down ash on the Manchester's home in Portland, OR. The diary entries from June of 1980 chronicled the many cleaning activities at 222 East Main.

Elmer was not a packrat. He and Mom cleaned out the farm buildings where Elmer had lived and worked for many years as well as Mom's house at 222 E. Main Street. Elmer was dealt a major blow when his stepdaughter from his first marriage, Fern, told him on July 2, 1980, that she intended to sell the farm. Elmer had no claim to the property. He had worked most of his life for Fern's dad. He married Emma, who was bedridden after her husband died so as not to be homeless. He cared for Emma until her death, shortly before his marriage to my mom.

After an exhausting couple of months, the couple enjoyed a special trip traveling west to see the older Sanford girls. The trip started on August 4th with the first stop in Portland to celebrate Barb and Art's 18th anniversary. Sister Shirley came down from Canada with her kids and a great time was had by all with the new grandpa reveling in his enjoyment of his new found family. The trip ended on August 22, 1980 with a stop at the Minnesota state fair, another in the series of firsts for Elmer. He was a simple man who worked as a farm laborer and had previously never been able to have the free time or money available to travel. Sadly, when they arrived home, they discovered that the house and garage had been broken into and the mower, a necessary tool for his lawn care business, had been stolen.

Rod and I came for a visit in September and made the rounds of the relatives showing off our daughter with Elmer basking once again in the glow of the family togetherness.

Rather than trying to repair the damage done to the sorry structure we called a garage that had been burglarized during the robbery they decided to build a new garage. The diary entry on October 1, 1980, indicated they "signed on the dotted line" for a package deal from Tomlinson's lumber. There were several mentions of how work on the garage was progressing as well as the usual delivering meals, working the phone at the center, and enjoying bus trips from the center to places like the West Acres Mall in West Fargo.

The fall was busy getting the garage under the roof before the winter.

In the fall when school supplies were purchased, there was a new offering from the beloved Minnesota Mining and Manufacturing Company known as 3M, the Post-it® Note. The new year of 1981 started as pretty much all before with the Rose Parade. The thing that was different about Mom's diary was it had also become a financial ledger with records of checks cashed and bills paid. Amounts recorded were precise, down to the penny. Mom took on these duties at home for the first time after Dad died and she continued as Elmer could not read or write. It was a somewhat natural transition as Mom had always done bookkeeping for the various organizations she was affiliated with and only Daddy seemed to consider her incapable. The pipes still froze but Mom had a note "Elmer just takes care of things, such a relief!" February 16, 1981, Mom noted "our ten-month anniversary". The first year of her remarriage was "good" with many mentions of "it is so good to be together" in the diary. The couple spent their first anniversary on a trip west with many of the same stops as in August but this time it included a trip to Fern's house in California.

It seemed Elmer was always painting something or building shelves and I saw the welcome transformation that he made in the house. He was also an avid gardener. He started his tiny plants from seeds in the house in egg cartons and knew just when and where to plant each plant to the best advantage. He cultivated beautiful flowers and healthy plants. He was rewarded for his efforts with bounty from a garden that he shared with all. He kept his car very clean and in good repair. He took his car to the shop. Mom noted, "car fixed $16.36". The next year of their marriage flew by and their 2nd anniversary in 1982 was marked by a "quiet celebration at home". Mom and Elmer made a Christmas trip to Illinois on the train. Their gift was an electric garage door opener. It was pronounced "the perfect gift" by Mom in her diary. They arrived home at 3 in the morning with the precious garage door opener which the railroad employees loaded into their car at the station. On January 5, 1983, Elmer put up the garage door opener.

Elmer's culinary specialty seemed to be vegetable soup and it was enjoyed with gusto by whoever came by. Their dietary habits were somewhat questionable as it seemed that the Red Owl grocery store had donut holes and coffee specials for seniors on Wednesday and despite Elmer's diabetes that seemed to be a staple breakfast each week. The A&T had hot dogs and coke on Thursday. Pie, just pie, was a frequent meal. Both of the Schimming pair were sick and unable to celebrate their 3rd anniversary. They were also becoming increasingly ecumenical with attending Golden Agers at the Lutheran Church, the Holy Rosary festival fundraisers religiously, as well as routine attendance at the films sponsored by the 1st Baptist Church. These activities usually included a potluck and my mother usually noted jello as her contribution. June 30, 1983, the end of the fiscal year for the churches and other organizations had a note from Mom "Thank you Lord for a good day of business". In July, Hugh brought Mom and Elmer to Canton which was a tradition from years gone by to celebrate Hub and Mom's birthdays, July 13th and July 28th, respectively.

August each year marked Turkey Days in Ulen, with various turkey delicacies devoured by the attendees. Crazy Daze was a summer sidewalk sale in Detroit Lakes. One of the WCTU committees that was active at festivals was the Home Protection Committee. They provided information about the impact of alcohol on the family and home. Ironically, I think they were usually located in the vicinity of the beer tent.

In the fall of 1983 attendance at the Nazarene church seemed to be fading away. Elmer's clients for mowing and handyman jobs were done on Sunday so Mom grew weary of attending on her own. She initially viewed religious programs beginning with *It Is Written* at seven and progressed through the morning. As time went on Sunday became her regular laundry day if the weather suited. Her diary reflected the Sabbath keeping in a new way such as buying gas and making all preparations before sundown on Friday with no work time till after sundown on Saturday. In her diary, she noted numerous times "ready for the

Sabbath." She began to assume more responsibility at the S.D.A. She led the singing in the opening exercises for Sabbath school and only on one occasion did she report that she misspoke and said Sunday school rather than Sabbath school. She continued to sing solos such as "A Child of the King" and one week sang the song at both the Adventist and Nazarene churches. Each week there was a rhythm of working at the center answering the phones, delivering dinners, taking friends and neighbors to doctor appointments.

Rummage sales were an ecumenical activity, regular events at several area churches, the Congo (Congregationalist), Methodist, Episcopal, Catholic, and several brands of Lutheran. The churches seemed to have a tacit agreement that they didn't have their sales at the same time. The Congo was preferred as their members were generally wealthy businessmen married to women who had a fashion sense. Mom told me on one occasion when dismissing a rummage sale "There won't be any good things there as that church is just a bunch of farmers whose wives are really farm workers and mothers of the flock of the other farm hands. Everything is either worn out or out of style." The private rummage sales were prioritized by neighborhood with those in the south of town near the lake given priority as they were likely to have the "best stuff". There was a careful strategy for which sales to attend based on opening time and deals at the end "R. sale days today started at Congo 8am then Lincoln Avenue and returned at 1p to Congo for $1 bags."

In the first three years of their marriage, it was often recorded that boxes were taken to the community service arm of the Adventist church for giveaway. Once the farm and the house on East Main were cleaned out, Elmer and Mom seemed to morph from donators to almost weekly customers at the giveaway.

Anniversary and birthday celebrations were a frequent activity on a Saturday or Sunday afternoon. Usually on weekdays the funeral and dinner following were the highlights worthy of diary notations such as "good dinner". On busy days Mom would go to the funeral home and sign the book before going on to her responsibilities at the center. November 20, 1983, "TV blacked out" was noted in the diary, and on the following day, "New Quasar TV $408.10." Gone were the days of Dad trying to fix the TV. "Rough slippery weather" was noted on the 22nd but fortunately the couple had their beautiful new TV in time to watch the Macy's parade. In December several Christmas brunches and dinners were canceled due to the "ugly" weather and Mom rejoiced in having the TV as solace. The Heinze quartet was making the journey from Illinois and left on the 23rd expecting to arrive early afternoon. Highway 94 was closed for the first time in history. Rod and I spent a frightening afternoon of driving before we ended up in the last available room at the Holiday Inn in Wilmar, Minnesota. We spent two nights there with kind community members bringing in food for those of us who were stranded. Rod's new beautiful white Rivera disappeared under the snow and the engine was encased in snow and refused, understandably, to turn over until we were able to get assistance to start it around noon on Christmas day. We made a drive-by to friends we were supposed to have spent the night with on the 23rd and arrived in Detroit Lakes at six-thirty in the evening, then left on the 29th. We enjoyed skiing once the temperature rose above 20 degrees below zero. It was to be our first, last, and only winter family trip to Minnesota. We had a memorable argument about driving on the ice to visit my cousin at his ice-fishing palace on the lake. Rod held his ground about endangering the lives of our children. On December 30, 1983, Mom wrote "seems lonesome without the Heinze's."

1984 began as usual with the parades and were "so much better on the new TV".

Mom had a spell of vertigo at the end of January that interfered with all activities including church attendance. Picking up government commodities was a regular notation followed by grocery shopping to round out the things needed to cook when they weren't eating donuts, pie, or hot dogs on the local specials. On the fourth anniversary of their marriage, the happy couple went to the farm and home show. In May 1984, the couple drove the 378 kilometers in the gently used green Cadillac Hugh had purchased for them. The occasion was Rolland Alho's wedding in Winnipeg, Manitoba, Canada. Rolland was daughter Shirley's nephew Mom had enjoyed so much on the trip to Western Canada several years before. Mom noted that Elmer received a Father's Day card from Shirley in June. There were frequent trips to Hawley to visit Hazel, often picking up Harry on the way to enjoy lunch at the Hawley Senior Center together. The phone line in Hawley was on the same exchange as Mom's sister Evelyn and several other relatives in the Fargo/Moorhead area so calls were made at no cost from Hazel's home. Sometimes, Hazel and Harry would accompany the couple on additional visits once they knew the people were home, or, the calls might have been to share information only. In August and September eating fresh corn on the cob was an acceptable complete meal option, especially on the days when the corn was being prepared and packaged to freeze. Apple juice and zingers at $1.69 masqueraded as a meal a few times. Pancakes eaten at home or Perkins were appropriate for breakfast, lunch, and dinner, a few times up to three times the same day.

Other monthly activities mentioned were the Emmanuel Nursing Home Auxiliary, Christian Women's Club, Joy Club, and the Jaycee who sponsored the mid-summer water carnival. Volunteer fire companies in the area battled it out in water fights, a fan favorite. A tour of lake homes provided an afternoon of enjoying vistas of the fall foliage and some delightful treats. Mom's filling came out of an important molar at a 1984 Halloween feast. A new dentist got her in and replaced the filling for $11.40 the next morning. Mom was diligent in her work schedule at the center but did take off on November 11, 1984, as Nan and Andy Bishop, Shirley's sister and brother-in-law came for a visit. Thanksgiving Day dinner was enjoyed at the Zion Lutheran fellowship hall. December 1984 was highlighted by all the organizational parties and traditional foods such as torsk, poached and broiled cod with butter, and lutefisk. Torsk I have had and enjoyed it, but lutefisk is a different story. My Danish ancestors never got on the lutefisk bandwagon and my father being from English stock didn't lean in the lutefisk direction. Several times Mom's sisters' Norwegian husbands dragged us to the Sons of Norway dinners. Elmer, though of German descent, lived and worked

Life After Vance (1979-1993)

with Norwegian families most of his life so he was a great fan of lutefisk. Lutefisk was never mentioned in the diary until the Elmer years.

Several sources recount a Viking legend about the creation of lutefisk. During a battle fish drying on tall birch racks were burned. Months later hungry Vikings were sustained when they found the remnants of that fish. As romantic as that may sound, in my estimation, it does not give proper justification to continue to consume the gelatinous version of fish unless you were truly starving. It has been traditional Scandinavian holiday fare since the Middle Ages when there was active trade in the nutrient-rich dried fish. Now the folks that live in Scandinavian countries have pretty much kicked the lutefisk habit. The use of lutefisk is pretty much limited to feed tourists who want to enjoy authentic foods when traveling. Far more lutefisk is consumed in the United States by Scandinavian Americans in Lutheran churches and the Sons of Norway Lodge. Madison, Minnesota, just a little south of Detroit Lakes, declared itself the lutefisk capital of the world in 1982. Reportedly, the 1,500 or so residents of this 1.2 square mile community consume more lutefisk per capita than anywhere else on the planet.

You need to be dedicated to eating lutefisk as it takes two weeks of preparation before it is ready to cook. First, the dried fish must be soaked for six days in cold water, with the water changed daily. The lutefisk is then soaked in a solution of cold water and lye for two days without changing the solution. When this treatment is finished, the fish saturated with lye is inedible. To make the fish edible, a final treatment of yet another six days of soaking in cold water, changed daily, is needed. In truth, the fact that lye is used in the reconstitution might have been a tradition started by accident. Ash from the fires may have gotten into the pots where the dried fish was soaking and it was discovered that the dried fish with the ash contamination soften up faster. The tradition continues despite the difficulty in now acquiring the dried fish and the whole reconstitution process. To cook the fish to avoid it from falling to pieces a layer of salt is put over it for 30 minutes or more to allow the saturated fish to release the water. It is then rinsed off, steam-cooked in a pan with a tight lid for 25 minutes at a low temperature. It is traditionally served with boiled potatoes, mashed peas, melted butter, and small pieces of fried bacon.

The days in December noted gift wrapping as well as cards sent and received. Mom always bought a stockpile of gifts ahead of time and selected just the right one for whatever occasions and people they associated with during the holiday season. Christmas dinner at the Vo-tech school on Christmas day had a traditional plain old USA menu and was pronounced: "good".

1985 started off with the traditional Orange and Rose Bowl Parades. On the 3rd Mom said she felt "draggy" which continued for a week until the 10th. Elmer carried on all the household responsibilities for the week. On the 11th she rose and enjoyed the food for the first time but still felt "hung over". On the 12th she got up and went to church with Elmer on the morning of the Sabbath and her normal activities seemed to resume at that point: working at the center, doing business such as checking on insurance and paying bills, and "running around town". Her proudest accomplishment was taking W.C.T.U. materials to the Moorhead State University library in Moorhead and making an official presentation for them to be part of the library collection.

March 31, 1985, Mom wrote "put Easter notes on Bunny paper and mailed in time to arrive by Easter". Elmer had a doctor's appointment on April 3rd. My mother-in-law and sister-in-law made the trip to Minnesota with the kids and me and there was egg dying and hunting. Elmer was the star with his charming ways spoiling us all. Easter was April 8th. We headed back toward Illinois after church. On April 16, 1985, Mom simply wrote "Our 5th anniversary. Elmer got cancer report from Dr". The diagnosis was Colon Cancer. X-rays and tests were completed on the 17th in preparation for surgery. I returned on the 18th to be there for the surgery on the 19th. Elmer was "holding his own" but was in ICU for several days. Shirley came on the 20th and I left to go home on the 23rd. Shirley chauffeured Mom around to see Elmer and take care of everything. He came home from the hospital on the 29th. On the 30th she wrote, "Elmer making great gains". On May 1st, a Wednesday, they enjoyed coffee and donut holes at the Red Owl, a signal that the normal litany of activities

Life After Vance (1979-1993)

had restarted. On the 28th Mom wrote "#1 anniversary 52 years ago". June 11th the diary entry read "$500 to St. Mary's. Elmer is to come back in one year. Ate at Bonanza to celebrate". I could almost hear her heave a sigh of relief. In July, Hugh, Mom, and Elmer came to Canton for the birthday celebrations. Mom noted on the 13th, "Hugh's 48th". On the way back they stopped in Burlington, Iowa, to visit with Mom's Aunt Nellie. Barb and Art made their August visit before they would be heading back to school. The fall passed into a snowy November and Mom commented "Elmer keeps the snow under control beautifully". On December 13, 1985, amid the busy holiday preparation season, Mom noted "Elmer painful swollen foot." Elmer got into the clinic on the 16th and the Dr. performed "surgery" and gave him penicillin. Once again Christmas dinner was enjoyed at the Vo-tech. The start to 1986 was the usual but Mom noted they were a "bit behind" on work at home likely due to Elmer being slowed down a bit with his foot problem recovery still in progress. The big event of the spring was a trip to Hawaii and California from April 10, 1986, when Mom noted "turbulence over the ocean" to May 3, 1986, "home in the afternoon". Shirley and Howard had purchased a restaurant on the big island of Hawaii. The 6th anniversary was celebrated with a surprise party at the restaurant. The Hawaii portion of the tour included a pineapple farm, macadamia nut processing, and a volcano. The first-class flight to LA started the step-sibling competition for doing the best entertaining with Knotts Berry Farm, Disneyland, beach time, and the Crystal Cathedral. June 1, 1986, Mom wrote after having an opportunity to share about their trip with friends "I praise God that I can keep up & going." The summer passed with many visitors noted and a few bouts of vertigo several even occurring while in bed at night. I could hear Mom say "Oh bother!" just like Winnie the Pooh when faced with unpleasant situations. Sad news in August came from Dr. Nelson "Elmer is blind in his left eye". In September, either Mom or Elmer had a bout with the shingles but it wasn't clear in the diary. Mom went up to the Dakota clinic for testing and September 23, 1986, was the last diary entry. Mom had a stroke during the procedure and the familiar frightening process of life in the ICU waiting room began again. I have no actual dates of when all the events proceeded and who came and went but it was horrifying to be reliving the events of Daddy's last days. Fortunately, Mom did not perish but was forever changed. At some point, she did recover enough to be cared for at Emmanuel Nursing Home in Detroit Lakes. She had a feeding tube and could not progress to speak or walk due to the location of the stroke she could not remember anything and woke up in a new world every day with the knowledge gained the previous day lost. With a 6-year-old and 10-year-old it was a challenge to make the over 1200-mile roundtrip, which we did every time there was a day off of school. When I conducted the cleanout which spanned approximately 19 months from the spring of 1987 through the fall of 1988, I took at least one vanload every month or so of what had been collected in the last three to four years. Hopefully, the items were put to good use by others once they were back to where much of it had originated, the S.D.A. giveaway. During the excavation, I found many of the things that were recorded in detail in the diary as purchased at rummage sales or obtained at the giveaway. There were also several retail favorites, like Pamida and White Drug. I know that I carted off to the giveaway the six blankets that were purchased as a bargain at Pamida still in the original bag.

Elmer watched the kids at home a good bit of the time while I was taking care of Mom. My former boyfriend's parents, Harvey and Marion Schlauderaff, who had raised nine children, loved my kids and would babysit so I could go to Elmer's doctor appointments with him. Harvey and Marion raised sheep. On one particular occasion while they babysat Harvey was taking the tails off the sheep. Rachel was out in the barn with Harvey watching and Adam was in the house with Marion discussing the horrors of what was occurring in the barn as he assisted in creating the delicious meal we would consume when we returned. On this March 1988 visit, we received a bad report that Elmer had liver metastasis from his colon cancer. Between this and his decreasing eyesight I realized that we needed to make different living arrangements.

After consultation with the siblings, it was decided that Mom and Elmer should be moved to Canton. I was determined that we were going to make renovations to our home and install a stairlift and handicapped-accessible bathroom to make a cozy apartment in our basement. My two sisters and brother were not thrilled but deferred to my desires. I went "up north" in April prepared to make arrangements to bring her home.

Upon my arrival, I met with the physical therapist, Mrs. Wilkie, to inform her of my intentions. Mrs. Wilkie, formerly Miss Hansen, my high school physical education teacher, was not happy. I had her now husband for chemistry and we had always been very close and had a congenial relationship. She insisted that I care for my mother for three days on my own before she would talk to me again. My mother was small weighing far less than 100lbs. Confident that my children were safe at home with their grandpa I agreed. That first day went pretty well and I smugly thought things were going okay. Day two went well although I was tired and when I returned home after my twelve-hour shift, I learned that although no one was injured there had been several altercations between my adorable children. On day three things took a turn for the worse in my caregiving routine. Mom had intestinal distress and I changed her bed five times before lunch. Things got so desperate at home that Elmer called. On the way back to the nursing home I realized that this was not a sustainable routine. I did not have to do the laundry; I did not have full responsibility for her care. I did not give Mom her medications or manage her feeding tube as I was not a licensed nurse in Minnesota. My back ached as although she was not heavy, she was easily distracted, and in mid-move to put her in her chair she would let go of me and I had to grab her to avoid a fall. I tearfully told Mrs. Wilkie at our three o'clock meeting "You were right". She provided support and encouragement for the search for a nursing home near our home in Illinois.

It was four o'clock in the morning when I herded my sleepy children into the car to make the 611-mile over ten-hour trip by bedtime. The kids had been through a lot in these few days and they had school tomorrow.

The very next day at work I received news that there was a new nursing home built one mile from our home and would be completed in September.

During the intervening months, there were still trips to Minnesota but I spared the children the trip whenever possible if family members and friends were able to care for them for a few days in Illinois. If that couldn't be arranged and the kids had to come with me, I would bring a babysitter along. Elmer's strength was failing and he could stay on his own but was not able to have responsibility for the children.

Arrangements were made to transfer the couple to Minnesota for the September opening. One complication was that Mom pulled out her feeding tube and resisted the replacement so strongly that it was allowed to be left out. Her oral feeding required a great deal of finesse but she was much more content. The downside was that Medicare would no longer pay for her treatment and care as it was custodial and not skilled according to the guidelines.

My brother had bought a van so he could take Mom for outings after her stroke. Unfortunately, the van gave up the ghost in late August so we made arrangements for a costly medical transport. They allowed Elmer to ride along with a few belongings arriving at the end of September.

Mom's funds were depleted with the cost of her care and not too long after she arrived in Illinois I needed to apply for Medicaid. This was a very distasteful process but the upside was I learned a great deal which I was able to share with the patients that I cared for as they navigated the process.

We made a suite for Elmer in our former laundry room in our home and we had many happy times till Thanksgiving time. The kids loved to have their grandpa there and would snuggle up with him in bed to watch TV after supper. Saturday mornings he would call out in his thick German accent "Do you want to come in and see the funny people?" He laughed right along with the kids all morning watching cartoons.

The routine was I would drop Elmer at the nursing home three days a week on my way to work in the morning and pick him up after work. Other days I would take him to appointments and we visited

Life After Vance (1979-1993)

Mom together. One afternoon, the administrator met me and said that Elmer was failing and although they were happy to have him there, they had given him a bed to nap in almost every day lately and he would qualify for admission under Medicare guidelines. The arrangements were made for his admission. He was only there about two weeks before he passed away on December 16, 1988. Our pastor conducted a brief service at the nursing home and I took Mom to the funeral home to see Elmer before we took him to Minnesota for a proper service for his friends and burial. Mom sobbed and the funeral director assisted me to get her to let go of him. It was a dark day for all of us. Hugh's free travel for his family benefits extended to transporting the body to Minnesota free of charge. The trip to Minnesota for the funeral began right after church when the kids finished their Christmas program. Rod was not able to attend due to his work schedule at the fire department. The kids and I ended up in a gym in Iowa two nights due to a snow storm so we arrived only hours before the funeral on Tuesday. Providentially, during the Medicaid application process, my brother had bought Mom's house so he was caring for it and that did not complicate the situation of what needed to be done in Minnesota. The Manchester and Metcalfe family were not able to make the trip. There were some light moments as cousins and I speculated what we would be served as the usual funeral fair was usually coffee and ham sandwiches, both forbidden for Seventh Day Adventists. We got to giggling and Thorwald Thorwaldson, the funeral director, invited us to use the family room. Mercifully, we were able to compose ourselves and were not thrown out of the funeral. The lunch was egg salad sandwiches and an unidentified "hot drink or cold drink" offered by the servers. The hot drink was likely a coffee substitute made from grain that had no caffeine and did not seem to be the favorite. The cold drink was a fruit punch with some type of sweetener, probably natural stevia that did not have the detrimental health effects of sugar, which was generally shunned by the avid Adventists.

Once we returned home there was a new rhythm with Mom. Without Elmer, we began trying to take Mom out for outings which began on Christmas Day 1988. The local medical transport company provided free transportation home. We had two steps up and while carrying her Rod and I nearly turned her over in the bushes so we decided before making any future attempts we would install a ramp. Most evenings I would go to the nursing home and feed her supper after I had fed whoever was home and started them on their homework. If Rod was not home to supervise, they would each take a plate made from our leftovers to the two widowed neighbors. Mary was a devoted Polish Catholic who had no children of her own. Mary was short and Adam was already taller than she was. Rachel was looking forward to the day when she would be. Mary had not graduated from high school and lived in Chicago where she married the love of her life, Donald. Donald died after a short illness. Rod taught her to drive so she could go to Mass every day. All her furniture was covered in clear plastic and still sported her silver Christmas tree on a rotating mirrored platform illuminated with colored spotlights in her front window. Adam would watch TV in the den at the end of her galley kitchen while Mary fed him treats. I had no illusions that he was doing his homework so I made sure I came home earlier on the evenings he went to Mary's house. Rachel would go to Mayme's. Mayme was a retired teacher and delighted in helping Rachel with her homework and supervised her piano practice. I would feed Mom supper and afterward, we would watch *Murder She Wrote*, one of her favorite programs, together. This was a good activity to share as her inability to speak was not an issue. I would take her to her room and after the aids put her to bed, I would pray with her and put a cassette tape of music she liked in the rugged tape recorder before leaving. Many Saturdays Rachel would accompany me and we three would eat lunch together and I would do Mom's nails in vibrant colors. Once we had the ramp installed, we would bring her home or out to the kids' activities at school or church. The idea of having a pet at a nursing home was just beginning and for Christmas that year we purchased a dog for the nursing home where Mom resided. The residents seemed to enjoy the dog, especially Mom, who would be sitting at the end of the hallway with a vantage point to enjoy the antics of the dog. It was

LIFE AFTER VANCE (1979-1993)

here I would get her to take her to the dining room. On the evening of January 29, 1993, I looked down the hall and Mom was slumped over against the tray of her geriatric chair. I thought she was tired and had fallen asleep. As I walked down the hall, I called to her but she did not rouse. When I reached her, I touched her and she was cool to my touch. I realized slowly her color was not good and she wasn't breathing. The subsequent events are not clear to me but someone came to my aid we got Mom into her room and waited till the proper individuals were notified and the funeral home picked up her lifeless body. The next days were a fog culminating in her funeral in Detroit Lakes on February 2nd.

The New Garage

Mom

Chapter 10
The Legacy of a Woman of Faith

The shock of Mom's departure from this life was mitigated by the absolute assurance that my mother was a woman of faith and is now enjoying her eternal reward. This would have seemed unlikely as Mom grew up in a family of non-believing non-churchgoers. Exactly how she came to serve the Lord is a mystery to me. I only knew her as a devout woman of faith. I would often hear her ask herself or others: What Would Jesus Do (WWJD)? That was the standard that she applied to each decision. Cultural norms held no sway over her but the eternal consequences of her choices were the focus. Sophia Bricker, a freelance writer, shed some light on the origin of the phrase in her December 29, 2021, article published on Christianity.com. Ms. Bricker pointed out that scripture includes numerous verses, which encourage believers to imitate and follow their Savior.

In addition, many Christians in history recognized the importance of emulating Christ, such as Augustine and Thomas a Kempis. Both John Wesley and Charles Spurgeon also saw the importance of following Jesus and developing Christlike attitudes and actions.

However, Charles Sheldon was the one who made the phrase more widely known through his sermons and famous 1896 book, entitled *In His Steps: What Would Jesus Do?* My mother had a copy of this book on her shelf. The novel tells the story of a homeless man who collapses in front of the congregation in front of a packed house of the gentry of

First Church after asking the question "What do you Christians mean by following the steps of Jesus?" Chapter two contains the pastor's challenge to the members on the next Sunday: "I want volunteers from the First Church who will pledge themselves, earnestly and honestly for an entire year, not to do anything without first asking the question, what would Jesus do?"

Despite all the tragedy my mom faced in her life she believed she was a much-loved child of God with a purpose despite whatever circumstances assailed her. She often quoted Romans 8:28 (KJV) "And we know that all things work together for good to them that love God, to them who are the called according to His purpose". The King James Version was the version that she would likely complete most of her memorization from but she was an avid student of the bible and used many tools, including commentaries and other translations, versions, or modern paraphrases of the Bible as they came out. Some more conservative folks believed that the King James Version was the only true version to use and that other versions or study aids were "tools of the devil". One poor ignorant soul stated "The King James Version was good enough for Jesus, Paul, and Silas so it was good enough for him!" Mother only smiled and did not launch into correcting her church friend on the fact that these heroes of the faith lived sixteen centuries before the King James Bible was written and did not speak English. And, that the Bible was actually originally written in ancient Aramaic! She just went on living according to Matthew 22: 36-39:

> [36] "Teacher, which is the greatest commandment in the Law?" [37] Jesus replied: "Love the Lord our God with all your heart and with all your soul and with all your mind.[38] This is the first and greatest commandment. [39] And the second is like it: Love your neighbor as yourself."

It is unclear to me how old I was when I began paying heed to my mother's habit of using pithy sayings. She had several trademark bits of wisdom and dispensed them liberally and repeatedly. The primary thing that I remember my mother saying often was a variation of a quotation from Howard Hendrix, an influential preacher she enjoyed listening to on the radio. "There are only two things that last forever, people and the word of God." A follow-up was her customary remark if someone was complaining about someone being worthless. Her rapid retort was: "Everyone has value, even if is to be a bad example!" She loved people and had great confidence that they could turn themselves around based on God's grace.

My mother wrote many notes in the margins of her bible and also underlined scripture. In addition, there were sermon notes and scripture references written on a menagerie of scraps of paper. She wrote in pencil and various ink colors expressing her love for the word of God. There was no consistency or organization to how her notes were stored. I'm sure she could never find any of those notes in the hoarding haven we called home even if she tried. She was a "live in the moment, the housecleaning can wait", kind of girl. The one place, I would say the most important place, that consistency reigned supreme was her unwavering love for and faith in God.

My mother was not an ivory tower girl who was above it all in her religiosity. She was well aware that the world was broken and messy. She was not oblivious but was virtually unoffendable by criticism from the hyper-legalist church folks who hoped to mold her into a more devout person, translation, like them. The church folks were also quick to say "I told you so!" when those in deep sin that she reached out to took advantage of her kindness. To the chagrin of the church folks Mother didn't seem to care if her expressions of God's love were unappreciated, rebuffed, misused, or abused. Choosing to be unoffendable is the best way to serve people of all types. Mom knew that it wasn't her job to restore. It was God's. She lived scripturally, loving and serving in her own quirky way with her confidence in God unshaken.

There are said to be over 170,000 words in the English language, but as I thought about how to describe Mom, only one word came to mind — special.

Maybe this is because many people have told me time and time again that "your mom is a special woman". The fact that it was repetitive didn't make it any less sincere ... or less true.

I think Mom's specialness came from the fact that much of what she did seemed superhuman, just like seeing Superman fly. Everyone on the outside was in awe by the way that she sacrificed herself and put her needs on the back burner.

But that is just how she loved.

The Bible tells us that love is the most powerful force in the world.

"For God so loved the world..." John 3:16

"Love never fails..." I Corinthians 13:8

"And the greatest of these is love..." I Corinthians 13:13

My mom and dad were both models of love for me and so many. And while Dad practiced a full and complete love, Mom was into extreme love. If there was an Extreme Sports League for Love, Mom would have gone pro (adapted from a eulogy for Phyliss Meadows presented by her son Mark at funeral on January 7th, 2023, used with permission).

My mother never took the Lord's name in vain but she did have a reputation for using strong language. Shit and asshole were used infrequently but without apology or remorse. No one would ever argue her vocabulary was offensive but descriptive and yes, perhaps even necessary in radical situations.

Mom and I would participate in the watch night service, an annual tradition at our church. Since Daddy smoked, and smoking was more sinful than television, and the six or more hours of the event was much too long for him to be without having a cigarette he never fully participated. Drinking alcoholic beverages was also a sin. My daddy was a teetotaler, not for religious reasons but due to frugality and love of his family. A number of alcoholics in his family had caused great harm to their families and brought themselves to financial ruin. He did subscribe to the philosophy that one drink often calls for another and there could be a family predisposition. My mother was a card-carrying member of the Women's Christian Temperance Union (W.C.T.U.). The watchnight service was the church-sanctioned alternative to having an evening of drunken revelry on New Year's Eve. Watchnight service began with a buffet supper at the church. The buffet consisted of many "hot dishes", translation, casseroles, and salads mainly consisting of sugary gelatin and mayonnaise with hardly a vegetable in sight. Some of the attendees went home after the meal, which included my dad if he ventured forth at all. He would generally drop off my mom and me and arrange for someone else to bring us home. A good portion of the brave souls in the flock stayed for an evening of games. After the games wound down a serious prayer time began around 11 p.m. Most everyone was praying all at once in loud voices seemingly vying for God's attention with the assumption that He was hard of hearing. I remember in earlier years thinking why did they need to talk so loudly?! The culmination was when the pastor called things to order and served communion at the stroke of midnight.

In later years, when we had Rev. Taylor as the pastor the youth group increased in number. Rev. and Sister Taylor, (a.k.a. Sherman and Edna to the adults) had three boys of their own. They carved out rooms to rent in the tiny basement of the parsonage. These rooms were rented to boys attending the nearby technical school. The real purpose was to supplement the pastor's meager family income but it caused the youth group to explode. Also, one of the larger families had five children who were teenagers in their clan at that moment. Rev. Taylor's oldest son, Rod, played the electric guitar and his middle son, Ed, the drums. This type of music was allowed after the old folks went home after communion. The youth enjoyed their music and more games and were served breakfast as their finale.

Mom loved music. If there were a theme song for my mother's life it would have been the old hymn, "Blessed Assurance", penned by Fanny Crosby. Even now I hear her beautifully clear and resonant soprano voice belting out the chorus in my memory: "This is my story; this is my song. Praising my Savior all the day long!" Indeed, this was her personal testimony. A contemporary Christian gospel song that I have thought of while writing my mom's story is "God Is in This Story" written by Katy Nichole in cooperation with Ethan Hulse and Jeff Pardo:

> God is in this story, God is in the details
> Even in the broken parts
> He holds my heart, He never fails
> When I'm at my weakest
> I will trust in Jesus
> Always in the highs and lows
> The One who goes before me
> God is in this story

She had a beautiful soprano voice and often sang solos in church. All three older siblings took piano and would play arrangements for six hands at church and recitals. Mother loved music and she insisted on my lessons until Mrs. Sealander told her to save her 50 cents as I had no talent for the piano. I could play all the right notes and did practice but it never sounded like music. I felt somehow less spiritual as the music and church life seemed so wedded together.

Mom was always on the lookout for good music and she happened on a song by Peter Scholtes. Peter wrote the hymn "They'll Know We Are Christians by Our Love" while he was a parish priest at St. Brendan's on the South Side of Chicago in the 1960s. At the time, he was leading a youth choir out of the church basement and was looking for an appropriate song for a series of ecumenical, interracial events. When he couldn't find such a song, he wrote the now-famous hymn in a single day. Mother was chastised for bringing that type of music into the church, something by a radical, and a Catholic no less. One of the things that my mother liked about the song was it mirrored the music of the Native Americans that lived in our area, then called the Chippewa tribe now referred to as the Ojibwa. There were basically no black people outside of the twin cities area of Minnesota so in rural Minnesota our choice of whom to discriminate against were those Native Americans that shared our streets. Prejudices abounded, drunken Indians and referring to women as squaws were some of the mild disrespectful words that were directed toward the people that were largely unknown. It was sort of an unwritten rule that we didn't have them in our church. Well, one day a new neighbor, Mrs. Mayberry, a Chippewa, accepted Mom's invitation to church. Mom became godmother to all nine of her children and even Jeannette when they were baptized. Sometime later, when Jeanette Mayberry's husband, John, received news that he had inoperable cancer, he did the honorable thing according to his culture. He went out in the woods, so as not to leave a mess, and took his own life. Mom and the church people rallied to the support of the family and they became knitted into the fabric of the church and were lifelong friends.

The life of our household revolved around the church in a pleasant, predictable way. Regular church services were held three times a week: Sunday morning, Sunday evening, and Wednesday evening. The main extra church activities in which we partook were Nazarene Foreign Missionary Society (N.F.M.S.), Cradle Roll, and rotating prayer meetings held in various homes called The Hour of Power.

Mom had a typewriter and would type the church announcements to take to the local paper regarding regular weekly services and special events. She also performed the typing of official minutes and banking services for the church and other community organizations she belonged to. She was also the mistress of mailing with the proper labeling, packing, size and weight restrictions and could make sense of the most complicated customs forms. She was an educated, articulate woman and was comfortable performing these official business tasks. Mom was a "classy" lady who was well dressed and comfortable in a variety of settings. She was also a humble servant who would clean the church when necessary.

Mom was the president of the N.F.M.S and chairman of the Cradle Roll. As president of the missionary group, she gave the prescribed missionary lesson each month on the first Sunday evening, promoted reading of books written by the missionaries, was on the church board by virtue of office, coordinated special services where actual missionaries spoke, and promoted giving to support the missionary work. She also had the privilege of interpreting a denominational change from the title for the missionary arm of the church from Nazarene Foreign Missionary Society to the more politically correct Nazarene World Missionary Society (N.W.M.S.). Some held the belief that change, especially progress, was bad and was "moving us toward worldliness, and away from the Lord! "

The Alabaster Offering was taken by a musical procession to open Alabaster boxes into a container placed on the altar of the church on two Sunday mornings each year: one in February and one in September. The Alabaster Offering consisted mainly of coins. Individuals are challenged to regularly contribute the cost of small items, such as a candy bar, they desired but did not need to their Alabaster box. The boxes also served as reminders to pray for those people who would benefit from Alabaster buildings. According to the Church of the Nazarene website, the Alabaster Offering provides funds for property and buildings around the world. "While we understand the church consists of the people of God and not a building, buildings erected for the purpose of ministry help provide a sense of permanence, functionally enhance ministry efforts, and convey an attitude that the Church of the Nazarene intends to put down roots." Part of the joy of being the child of the missionary president was fully participating in every aspect of the missionary society, including the assembling and distribution of the Alabaster boxes and of course maintaining contributions to my own. The boxes were printed on flat cardboard and were about 6"x2"x2" with the top folding over with side flaps tucked down into the box which had a coin slot in the top and was secured by a sticker. The box was printed with a faux marble pattern to commemorate the loving anointing with oil that Jesus received on several occasions described in the gospels, poured from an alabaster container. There was a gold seal which held the flap down. Mother, being the wise woman that she was, knew that that sticker wasn't going to keep anyone from pilfering from the Alabaster box during the months it was in their home. In our home, Mom enforced the Zacchaeus method of repayment straight from the scripture. If I decided to get any money out of my box the repayment scheduled was pretty steep as recorded in Luke chapter 19. Zacchaeus the wealthy chief Tax Collector met up with Jesus when he was passing through Jericho. Jesus invited himself to Zacchaeus' home, to the usual chagrin of the religious leaders. Jesus' visit resulted in Zacchaeus becoming a changed man. Verse 8 gives credence to his repentant spirit when Zacchaeus stood up and said to the Lord, "Look, Lord! Here and now, I give half of my possessions to the poor, and if I have cheated anybody out of anything, I will pay back four times the amount." You guessed it, if I took a quarter out of my box, my mother would expect that I return a whole dollar. She was also in the habit of lifting my box as she passed by to encourage me with the words "feeling a little light to me" so I was careful to replace the quarter I might purloin from my box with four quarters rather than a paper dollar. I also found using pennies and nickels was a good strategy to beat Mom at her own box-lifting check game.

Boxwork, one of the especially important aspects of missionary society effort, was sending boxes containing practical items that missionaries needed to succeed in their tasks on the field that were not available or very expensive in the country where they were called to minister. One of the missionaries our church supported with our practical arts served at a leper colony in Africa. The ladies of the church brought their sewing machines and stitched together and rolled literally miles of bandages for the poor souls receiving treatment at the leper colony.

As Cradle Roll Chairperson Mom would take a small gift from the church to babies born at our local hospital. During her visit she invited the parents to bring their baby to church. Through the Cradle Roll program many regular attenders and members of the church initially came to church at Mother's invitation.

The church provided alternatives to many "worldly" activities throughout the year. The church frequently offered something special for Valentine's Day that often included all ages. Valentines were exchanged and my mother used the opportunity to fundraise for the N.W.M.S. She had valentines available at the back of the church the Sunday before Valentine's Day and asked for a donation of what they would have spent elsewhere. Mom would purchase the valentines at a hefty reduction the year before or in her thrift store rummage sale rounds. Her clientele built up over the years as they liked the fact that they could pick out individual cards and didn't have to commit to a pack of 36 with only 6 different designs. The customers were usually generous as they bantered over the stock she had and remarked "This is better than last year, Eva. Wherever did you find these gems?"

Easter activities were limited due to the fact that there wasn't a lot of pageantry associated with our denomination. We had a small choir for some of the years but sometimes no one to play the piano. Also, the weather in March and April did not lend itself to planning as a blizzard could spoil the plans.

The Christian alternative to spring prom provided by conservative churches in the area was pre-em. The abbreviation pre-em stood for the pre-eminence of Christ in the lives of the young people who attended. It was held once a year, and was open to all of the young people in the local congregations. Did I forget to mention that dancing is a sin? I got well acquainted with a number of students from other churches, whom I might have otherwise not met, when we sat together in study hall instead of going to P.E. when the activity was square dancing. Oftentimes, we subsequently socialized outside of school at many church-sponsored activities, including pre-em.

As all good church people do, first we ate. The difference was the tables were decorated with a theme and the food was served by waiters and waitresses, instead of the customary potluck. The wait staff was composed of willing or coerced church attenders. You could tell those who were there under duress by their tortured expressions. The unhappy ones' dark moods were exacerbated by the fact that they dressed alike, or at least similarly, according to the theme. Many of the looks were not flattering to anyone and usually involved some sort of element of handmade embellishment that was uncomfortable and somewhat fragile so it required constant adjustment. Since there was no dance there were generally skits, games, or singing. The acoustics of the venue, the church basement, had no sound system. Also, it was difficult to compete with the frenzied cleanup crew crashing dishes in the kitchen to get home to milk or do other chores.

The church honored all mothers on Mother's Day as well as those special cases such as oldest mother, youngest mother, and the mothers with the most children and grandchildren. The gift was usually the start of a single petunia broken from the plastic 12-pack. The twelve-pack was generally sufficient for the small congregation although Mr. Kiihn, who had a beautiful yard, planted with petunias, would have an extra one just in case a busload of mothers on their way to an unknown location broke down and would happen into the church on Mother's Day morning. There were only 13 voting members over 15 years old in our tiny church so even the one flat of twelve plants showed considerable optimism.

The month of June usually began with vacation Bible school at the church immediately following the end of the school year. In the later years of this five-year period, it seemed that school activities had crept into the first week of June and Bible school was delayed a week or moved to the week before school began again in the fall.

The only other things her diary mentioned about church through the summer were the regular monthly and special board meetings. During the summer of 1964 there were frequent meetings of the board to select a new pastor. One particular entry was poignant for me as Mom wrote as if straight from her pen to God's ear, "This is a hectic and hard time of trial. We want and need God's leadership". The rest of the summer the church's social calendar was dormant to allow the natural course of events on the farm and tourist industry to unfold.

The kick-off to the fall church schedule was revival. Services were held each evening for a week or two with sermons and special music by a traveling evangelist. There would be an altar call and many people would go to the altar every night convicted about something they needed to confess. It was important to get these meetings in during September or October, since the summer was sometimes referred to as the season of sin. The months running around in skimpy bathing suits assaulted by sinners from around the world took its toll on a person's soul. It was critical to have revival completed and be spiritually refreshed and rooted in the faith ready for Halloween, "the devil's holiday". Some churches offered an All-Saints Day celebration, on November 1st where attendees came dressed as bible characters, translation, came wrapped in a sheet or a bathrobe with sandals. The cleverest among them might add a prop such as a sling, to make their identity clearer. This lasted only a few short years until eventually the children were allowed to partake in actual Halloween as long as they wore costumes that were not gruesome, demonic or related to witchcraft. Somehow ghosts seemed to be acceptable.

Thanksgiving celebrations were left to family and the church did not interfere. The exception might be someone who did not have family that came to the church. A person who may have been on his/her own who attended church might be invited to a family celebration: Hebrews 13:2 "Be not forgetful to entertain strangers: for thereby some have entertained angels unawares."

Christmas was a big production with the retelling of the Christmas story using some live animals at times. Due to the unavailability of a camel (camels are NOT indigenous to Minnesota!), most often a cardboard cutout was used. This was all performed using sheets as a curtain hung on a wire and opened manually. My dad was generally the innkeeper as his spiritual situation was questioned by many and none of them wanted to be the one to tell poor pregnant Mary there was no room in the inn.

At that time in Minnesota there was what was called Wednesday School or religious release time. Students would get out in the early afternoon and go to various churches to have religious instruction. In small churches like ours, it would be a handful of students instructed by the pastor. Larger Lutheran churches had impressive educational facilities, as well as, skilled educators that led the well-planned curriculum.

My mother, a master innovator, birthed the idea of having a class for retarded protestant children. The Catholic Church had a class for public school students who did not attend Holy Rosary School. The class for the protestant children was a joint project of the Association for Retarded Children (A.R.C.), the Parent Teacher Association (P.T.A.), and the Detroit Lakes Area Ministerial Association, usually referred to as the Ministerial Association.

Please note that *retarded* was the politically correct term at that time for individuals who were developmentally challenged. My mother adapted the curriculum from materials available and taught Wednesday school at the First Lutheran Church for all the retarded children from protestant families in the Detroit Lakes area. With her instruction and tutelage several of her students were able to achieve milestones such as being confirmed, receiving communion, or joining the church of their choice. She would always have a large class and felt like it was worth her time and efforts despite what others might have considered results small for her large investment.

Sharing books we were reading and recommending books to each other was one of the great joys of my relationship with my mother. This was especially true for Christian volumes that we heard about from church friends or on a radio program. Even though I believe that my mother is enjoying her eternal reward in heaven, I still miss her! While I was a new manager at a cancer center in southern Delaware, I experienced a very deep, intense longing for her to be there, with me, in this flesh and blood world. It was the umpteenth time after her death, but it was the worst and led to a night of crying and not sleeping. It was 2008, over 15 years after her death. I was sitting alone in the third-floor condo the hospital had provided. It was almost 8 p.m., a perfectly appropriate bedtime from my perspective. I had just arrived home and I was still supperless. Since it was the off-season my efforts to find a location to pick up a sandwich were fruitless. The knowledge that I likely had nothing of substance to fix deepened my longing for how Mom would have something ready for me to eat when I got home from work no matter what time it was. Maybe a bowl of oatmeal could suffice.

My sister, Shirley, who physically and emotionally most resembled my mom, had made the two-day, almost one-thousand-mile drive from Illinois with me. We looked like the Clampetts, with everything we stuffed into the 2003 blue Buick LeSabre. Hubby Rod, would join me at the end of May, a mere three months from now, driving our other car accompanying the truck that would contain the rest of our earthly belongings. The first three weeks Shirley filled my off-work hours with laughter and support. She did the cooking and because she was there, I didn't eat alone. I took her to the airport the last night and on the radio we heard about a book about praying for your adult children which sounded interesting. Before I fell into bed exhausted, I resolved that I would look for the book in the true Sanford tradition the next day. My Mom's primary rule in the protocol for obtaining a book was to look at the library first. On my lunch hour I called the library only to learn that since I was not a cardholder, they would not discuss with me whether they had the aforenoted book or not. They described the impossible for me requirements to obtain a library card. Since I was a temporary ward of the hospital, I could not produce the required utility or telephone bill with my name and address, or a Delaware driver's license. I then learned from the unhelpful librarian that the library had very limited hours and the location was impossible to get to at all if you had a job. The Department of Motor Vehicles accessibility was limited as well. I passed the afternoon a bit stunned by the reality that I wasn't in Kansas anymore. Climbing the ninety-seven dimly lit stairs on the windy rainy evening to the condo after my fourteen-hour day at the cancer center, I felt the separation from my mother in a new way. Finding my condo was not an easy job as it was at the back of a mixed housing development that was largely unoccupied this time of the year. More oatmeal and to bed.

That Sunday, I drove the two hours to go to church with my daughter and her family and to my delight discovered the book could be borrowed from the church library and I went home with it that afternoon.

The magic of that book was a real blessing and I began praying prayers for my beloved children adapted from that book.

I felt comfort in knowing that my mother had always prayed for me and it was part of her legacy. Mother's faith in God was the core of her existence. Although the activities of the church were important, she sought wisdom from God in her faith walk. A para church organization, Campus Crusade for Christ was formed in 1951. The purpose of the organization was to assist students in developing personal spiritual disciplines. Mother was a voracious consumer of their materials as they were very timely since Eva's oldest was about to go off to college. She took seriously the spiritual disciplines advocated and incorporated them into her routines. What a privilege to have this woman of faith as my mother.

Barbara's descendants

Left to right Aurora 3, Leila 5, and Caspian 9 weeks

Great-grandpa David, Dad- Dave, Catalina, Grandpa Eric Manchester

Shirley's descendants

L to R. 1st row: Gigi Shirley, Grandma Terri holding Caspian, Mom- Danielle
2nd row: Omar, Jameilo, Asher, Martin, Grandpa Michael, Dad- Nygel, Zeva

Starting at the top left working around the card clockwise:
Mabel (6) & River (10) Crooks; Leo & Ruby (2) Gosselin; Andrew & Jana; Mariah (6) & Remi (3) Critchley; Stella (19) & Sean (21) Crooks and the little dog Luna.

Sylvia's descendants

L Rod, Sylvia, Adam R Abby

Zora, Raleigh, Rachel, Rod

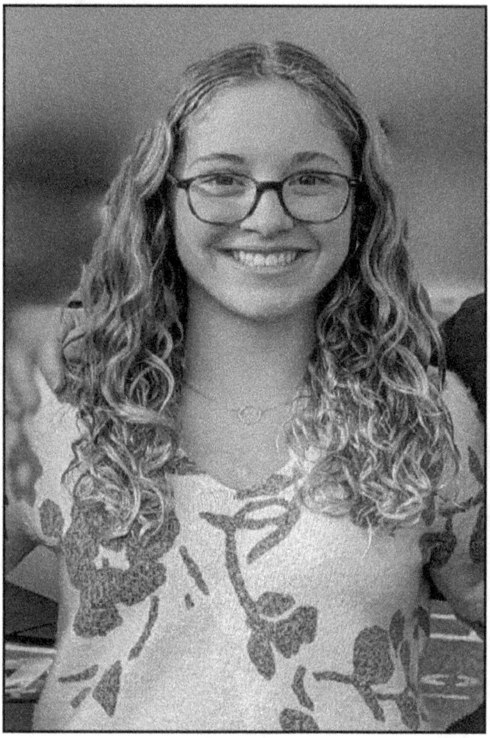

Bibliography

Anderson, Chester G., ed. *Growing up in Minnesota Ten Writers Remember Their Childhoods*—Minneapolis, Minnesota: University of Minnesota Press, 1976.

Brown, Foveaux Jess Lee. *Any given day*. New York, New York: Warner, 1997.

Cameron, Linda A. "Rural Electrification Administration in Minnesota." MNopedia, Minnesota Historical Society. http://www.mnopedia.org/thing/rural-electrification-administration-minnesota (accessed February 22, 2024).

Carey, Carlton. *Sven & Ole Jokes and More*. Atlanta, Georgia: Westwood Books Publishing LLC, 2019

Church of the Nazarene. Accessed February 27, 2024. https://nazarene.org/.

Dill, Emma. "Prairie Home Companion." MNopedia, Minnesota Historical Society. http://www.mnopedia.org/thing/prairie-home-companion (accessed February 22, 2024).

Grant, Lindsey. *READY, SET, MEMOIR!* San Francisco, California: Chronicle Books LLC, 2021.

"Howard Hendrix Quotations." A-Z Quotes. Accessed February 27, 2024. https://www.azquotes.com/.

Knudtson, Elisa. *History of Ulen Area in 75 Years of Progress*. Ulen, Minnesota: The Ulen Union, 1961.

Lewis, Sinclair. *Main street*. Digireads.com, 2018.

National Turkey Federation. Accessed February 28, 2024. https://www.eatturkey.org/.

"Orphan Trains: Placing out Children in Minnesota." Gail Family Library. Accessed February 22, 2024. https://libguides.mnhs.org/orphantrain/more.

"Significant Events of the 20th Century." Oxford Reference, 2012. https://www.oxfordreference.com/display/10.1093/acref/9780191735639.timeline.0001.

Taylor, Johua. "History of Hymns: 'They'll Know We Are Christians by Our Love.'" Discipleship Ministries, June 26, 2019. https://www.umcdiscipleship.org/articles/history-of-hymns-theyll-know-we-are-christians-by-our-love#:~:text=Peter%20Scholtes%2C%20a%20Catholic%20priest,sing%20(Daw%2C%20303).

Wikipedia contributors, "Ice cutting," *Wikipedia, The Free Encyclopedia*, https://en.wikipedia.org/w/index.php?title=Ice_cutting&oldid=1206444577 (accessed February 22, 2024).

Wikipedia contributors, "Lake Wobegon," *Wikipedia, The Free Encyclopedia*, https://en.wikipedia.org/w/index.php?title=Lake_Wobegon&oldid=1189839427 (accessed February 22, 2024).

Wikipedia contributors, "Sven," *Wikipedia, The Free Encyclopedia*, https://en.wikipedia.org/w/index.php?title=Sven&oldid=1203417658 (accessed February 22, 2024).

Wikipedia contributors, "What Would Jesus Do?" *Wikipedia, The Free Encyclopedia*, https://en.wikipedia.org/w/index.php?title= What_would_Jesus_do%3F (accessed February 22, 2024).

Acknowledgments

Particular thanks go to two of my beloved first cousins, my aunt Evelyn's daughter, Joanne Ward, and Laura Jevning, my aunt Mayme's daughter, and my second cousin, Terry Larsen and his wife Elsie. These individuals provided useful information as well as encouragement and support. Terry and Elsie provided a particular local flare as they still live on the property owned by my Uncle Jim, my grandpa's brother, in the home they built. Their daughter lives at home with her parents but their two boys married and built their homes just down the road. Their property is near where my grandparents' farm was on Detroit Mountain. Elsie grew up "on the mountain" and she and her sisters came to our church and were strongly linked to my mom before her marriage to Terry.

Roseann, my editor, conscience, research assistant, and beloved friend worked tirelessly in the process of the book development

A childhood friend from our neighborhood, Patty Olson Sanaker, who has developed her expertise in genealogical research, blessed me with several documents after we had a conversation about my desire to portray events in my mother's story as accurately as possible. She also provided information about her family so that I could interpret and put the entries in my mom's diary in the correct context. Many of those entries related to her family or other neighbors.

Classmates from high school and other friends from the Detroit Lakes area took time to review the information when I made the trip for my class reunion in July of 2022. Particularly helpful were friends I grew up with in the church: Ed Taylor, Beverly Mastin Bell, and LaDonna York Olmstead.

Nancy Gallo, a work friend of my brother's, whom I have known for over half a century, agreed to give it a final read-over as she knew or has known most of the characters. Nancy moved to Minnesota when she accepted a job at Northwest Orient Airlines in 1965, which gave her a unique perspective on the Minnesota culture.

Thanks to all who invested in this project including the staff of Xulon Publishing who provided support to "finally make it happen".

Helpful Cousins

left: Lynn, Joanne and Bev right: Al and Laura

Elsie and Terry Larsen

Acknowledgments

Helpful Friends

Nancy Gallow

Patty Sanaker

LaDonna Olmstead, Ed Taylor, Sylvia, Bev Matin Bell